A Typology of Domestic Violence

THE NORTHEASTERN SERIES

ON GENDER, CRIME, AND LAW

Editor: Claire Renzetti

For a complete list of books available in this series, please visit www.upne.com

Drew Humphries, *Women, Violence, and the Media: Readings in Feminist Criminology*

Gail A. Caputo, *Out in the Storm: Drug-Addicted Women Living as Shoplifters and Sex Workers*

Michael P. Johnson, *A Typology of Domestic Violence: Intimate Terrorism, Violent Resistance, and Situational Couple Violence*

Susan L. Miller, editor, *Criminal Justice Research and Practice: Diverse Voices from the Field*

Jody Raphael, *Freeing Tammy: Women, Drugs, and Incarceration*

Kathleen J. Ferraro, *Neither Angels nor Demons: Women, Crime, and Victimization*

Michelle L. Meloy, *Sex Offenses and the Men Who Commit Them: An Assessment of Sex Offenders on Probation*

Lori B. Girshick, *Woman-to-Woman Sexual Violence: Stories of Women in Prison*

Karlene Faith, *The Long Prison Journey of Leslie van Houten: Life Beyond the Cult*

Jody Raphael, *Saving Bernice: Battered Women, Welfare, and Poverty*

Neil Websdale, *Policing the Poor: From Slave Plantation to Public Housing*

Lori B. Girshick, *No Safe Haven: Stories of Women in Prison*

Sandy Cook and Susanne Davies, editors, *Harsh Punishment: International Experiences of Women's Imprisonment*

Susan L. Miller, *Gender and Community Policing: Walking the Talk*

James Ptacek, *Battered Women in the Courtroom: The Power of Judicial Responses*

Neil Websdale, *Understanding Domestic Homicide*

Kimberly J. Cook, *Divided Passions: Public Opinions on Abortion and the Death Penalty*

Amy Neustein and Michael Lesher, *From Madness to Mutiny: Why Mothers Are Running from the Family Courts—and What Can Be Done about It*

Jody Raphael, *Listening to Olivia: Violence, Poverty, and Prostitution*

Cynthia Siemsen, *Emotional Trials: Moral Dilemmas of Women Criminal Defense Attorneys*

A TYPOLOGY OF DOMESTIC VIOLENCE

Intimate Terrorism,

Violent Resistance,

and Situational

Couple Violence

Michael P. Johnson

NORTHEASTERN UNIVERSITY PRESS

Boston

Published by University Press of New England

Hanover & London

Northeastern University Press
Published by University Press of New England,
One Court Street, Lebanon, NH 03766
www.upne.com
© 2008 by Northeastern University Press
Printed in the United States of America
5 4 3

University Press of New England is a member of the Green Press Initiative.
The paper used in this book meets their minimum requirement for
recycled paper.

Library of Congress Cataloging-in-Publication Data
Johnson, Michael P.
A typology of domestic violence : intimate terrorism, violent resistance,
and situational couple violence / Michael P. Johnson.
    p.   cm. — (Northeastern series on gender, crime, and law)
Includes bibliographical references and index.
ISBN-13: 978–1–55553–693–0 (cloth : alk. paper)
ISBN-10: 1–55553–693–X (cloth : alk. paper)
ISBN-13: 978–1–55553–694–7 (pbk. : alk. paper)
ISBN-10: 1–55553–694–8 (pbk. : alk. paper)
1. Family violence—United States.   2. Marital violence—United States.
3. Victims of family violence—United States.   I. Title.
HV6626.2.J64   2008
362.82′9201—dc22   2007052379

To my parents,

PAUL and DOROTHEA JOHNSON

Contents

Introduction 1

Chapter 1: Control and Violence in Intimate Relationships 5

Intimate Terrorism and Other Types of Partner Violence 7

Intimate Terrorism 7

Violent Resistance 10

Situational Couple Violence 11

Mutual Violent Control 12

Doing Research on Intimate Terrorism and Other Types of Partner Violence 12

Asking the Right Questions: The Nature of Coercive Control 13

Not Asking the Right Questions: The Battered Husband Fiasco 17

When the Right Questions Aren't Asked, Where Do We Find the Types? 23

Chapter 2: Intimate Terrorism: Controlling Your Partner 25

The Basic Characteristics of (Heterosexual Men's) Intimate Terrorism 26

Nonviolent Control Tactics 26

The Nature and Pattern of the Violence 29

Who Are the Intimate Terrorists? 30

Two Types of Intimate Terrorists: Psychological Commonalities and Differences 31

Risk Markers for Intimate Terrorism 33

The Effects of Intimate Terrorism 37

Economic Effects 38

Physical Health 39

Psychological Health 41

Effects on the Relationship with the Abuser 43

Incipient Intimate Terrorism/Nonviolent Coercive Control 46

Chapter 3: Fighting Back: Violent Resistance 48

Women Coping with Intimate Terrorism 48

Violent Resistance 51

Leaving 53

Desperate Acts 55

The Good News 59

Chapter 4: Conflicts That Turn Violent: Situational Couple Violence 60

Variability in the Violence Itself 61

The Causes of Chronic Situational Couple Violence 62

Sources of Couple Conflict 63

Couple Communication Patterns That Affect Escalation to Violence 65

Individual Background and Personality Factors That Affect

Escalation to Violence 67

The Effects of Situational Couple Violence 69

Physical Health 69

Psychological Health 69

The Relationship with the Abuser 70

The Essential Variability of Situational Couple Violence 70

Chapter 5: Implications for Intervention, Prevention, and Research 72

Implications for Intervention 72

Shelters and Other Battered Women's Services 73

Law Enforcement 75

Batterer Programs 78

Family Court and Child Protective Services 81

Coordinated Community Response 83

Implications for Prevention 83

Implications for Research 84

Appendix A:

Identifying Intimate Terrorism and Other Types of Partner Violence 87

Measuring Coercive Control 87

Identifying High Coercive Control 90

What Is the Role of Violence in the Typology? 91

The Data in this Book 91

Samples and Measures Used in the Analyses for This Book 92

Johnson et al.: Six Other Papers 94

Appendix B: Stalking and Separation-Precipitated Violence 102

Intimate Terrorism and the Risks of Leaving 102

Separation-Precipitated Violence That May Be
   Situational Couple Violence 103

Appendix C: Gender and Intimate Partner Violence 105

Gender and Intimate Terrorism 105

What About Situational Couple Violence? 107

A Note on Same-Sex Relationships 109

Notes 111

References 141

Index 155

A Typology of Domestic Violence

Introduction

I used to say I found the verbal abuse much worse than the physical abuse. Even though the physical abuse was terrible. Because I suppose it was only—only!? God—once, twice a year. It was the constant verbal [attacks] that used to get me down more than anything. Cause that's how you lose your self-esteem. But the violence is awful, the violence is terrible. I think you've got to take that, though, as part of it. If you're constantly being told you are a useless jerk, to be [beaten] just . . . compounds it.[1]
—A formerly battered woman

The horrors of domestic violence are now all too well known and are regularly addressed in the mass media.[2] Most of us have seen movies about domestic violence, or watched an episode of our favorite television drama that dealt with the issue, or seen it discussed on talk shows, in general interest magazines, or in the daily news. But is domestic violence perhaps an isolated problem that occurs only very rarely in U.S. families? On the contrary, in the United States,

- 2–6 million women experience violence from their male partners each year.[3]
- 25–30 percent of women who come to emergency rooms for injuries are there for domestic violence–related problems.[4]
- Over 1,000 women were murdered in the year 2004 by their husbands or boyfriends.[5]

Domestic violence is not one of those extremely rare family horrors (such as a grandfather who sleeps with his grandson's girlfriend) that is blown all out of proportion by the selective programming of shock-addicted talk show producers. It is clear that domestic violence is not at all unusual. It is a serious and far-reaching social problem.

The numbers presented above were chosen to document the severity of the problem of domestic violence, but they also illustrate the two great debates in research on intimate partner violence. The first debate is about gender and domestic violence. A critic might ask of the numbers above, "Why are you ignoring battered husbands? There is plenty of reputable social science evidence that wives are as likely to beat their husbands as vice versa." The conventional answer to this challenge has been that such evidence is flawed, and that there are truly reputable studies showing that virtually all domestic violence is perpetrated by men. My answer—and the central theme of this book—is that there is more than one type of intimate partner violence: some studies address the type of violence perpetrated primarily by men, while others are getting at the kind of violence that women are involved in as well. My research demonstrates that in heterosexual relationships the violence that I call "intimate terrorism" is perpetrated almost entirely by men, not women. And, as you will see in chapter 1, intimate terrorism refers to the sort of violence that most people think of when they think about "domestic violence," the kind of violence described above by a battered woman. Her partner beat her, humiliated her, attacked her through a variety of tactics, both violent and nonviolent, that allowed him to control her behavior. This pattern of coercive control is largely, though not exclusively, perpetrated by men.

The second major debate involves how many women are abused each year by their partners. A critic might exclaim that the estimates presented above range from two to six million: "Can't you be more precise than that? Is it two million or is it six million?" The answer, once again, comes from the central theme of this book. If there is more than one type of intimate partner violence, then the numbers depend on what type you're talking about. Six million female victims each year is a reasonable estimate for what I call "situational couple violence," but this type of violence is not what most people are thinking of when they ask about domestic violence. It does not involve the systematic, controlling abuse that we associate with "battering," or "wife beating." If intimate terrorism, involving systematic, controlling abuse, is what we mean by domestic violence or battering, then the best estimate is that somewhere around two million women a year are battered by their husbands or male partners in the United States.

The distinctions that I make among types of violence are as much about control as they are about violence. Other feminist researchers have pointed out the dangers of focusing narrowly on violent *acts* while ignoring the broader relationship context within which the violence takes place.[6] They have argued persuasively for the need to see such violence as one piece of a more general pattern of power and control.[7] My feminist approach, rather than seeing all intimate partner violence as involving a general pattern of control, distinguishes among types of violence on the basis of the control context in which they are embedded. Intimate terrorism is violence embedded in a general pattern of coercive control. It is the violence that we encounter most often in shelter populations, in emergency rooms, and in law enforcement. In heterosexual relationships, it is perpetrated almost entirely by men, and it has been the basis of most feminist theories about the nature of domestic violence. It has a completely different dynamic than does situational couple violence, a type of violence that is not about general control, but comes from the escalation of specific conflicts. General social surveys uncover mostly situational couple violence; they have been the source of most family violence theories about the nature of domestic violence.[8] And neither of these two types of violence looks much like the violent resistance that we see among women trying to cope with intimate terrorism.

The research literature on domestic violence is full of misunderstandings and disagreements that come from the failure to make such distinctions. The longstanding and often rancorous debate regarding the gender symmetry of domestic violence is an excellent example.[9] Feminist theorists, studying primarily intimate terrorism, insist that domestic violence is perpetrated by men against women; they present evidence from agency samples to back up their theoretical arguments. Family violence theorists, studying primarily situational couple violence, insist that women are as violent as men in intimate relationships; they present evidence from general surveys to back up their theoretical arguments. Until recently, neither group has considered the possibility that they are simply studying two different phenomena.[10]

My goal in this book is to consider what we know and what we don't know about these different types of intimate partner violence. Although I can draw from more than twenty-five years of systematic research on domestic violence, most of this work has not made the necessary distinctions.[11] As a result, we have been trapped in overgeneralizations that assume that intimate partner violence is a unitary phenomenon. My strategy for "taking apart" these overgeneralizations is two-fold. The clearest evidence will come from recent research that does make the necessary distinctions and that provides direct tests of hypotheses about the differences among types of intimate partner violence. It is also possible, however, to make good use of research that does not explicitly address these necessary distinctions. Certain clues help to identify research that can reasonably be argued to offer evidence relevant primarily to one type or another of intimate partner violence. And there are also analyses in this older literature that make distinctions (such as those between "mild" and "severe" violence) that can provide clues as to which generalizations apply to which types of violence.

This typological approach is relatively new, first proposed in 1995 and only recently becoming the focus of research designed to test its implications. Thus, at this point in the development of scientific research on the different types of domestic violence, we may not find definitive answers. As you will see, however, we do already know quite a bit. Although we may not have all the details worked out yet, it is clear that the different types of intimate partner violence develop in different ways during the history of a relationship, and that they have quite different consequences. There is also evidence that they have different causes, and that they therefore require different interventions, both at the individual level and in the development of general social policy. The task ahead—developing a theoretical framework that recognizes these differences—will involve the complex scientific process of theory development and empirical testing, followed by theory revision and further testing. But we have enough of a start in this process to know that it is time to stop talking about domestic violence as if it were a unitary phenomenon and start talking about what we know about the different types of violence in intimate relationships.

Control
and Violence
in Intimate
Relationships

One woman we interviewed told us that she was first beaten
on her honeymoon and when she cried and protested, her
husband replied, "I married you so I own you."[1]

In order to understand the nature of an individual's use of violence in an intimate relationship, you have to understand its role in the general control dynamics of that relationship. Some people use violence as one of many tactics in a general strategy aimed at taking complete control over their partner, as in the case of the newlywed husband quoted above. Others may become violent in order to resist their partner's attempts to control them. For still others, their violent behavior may have little to do with control. In this chapter I will distinguish among four types of intimate partner violence that are defined by the extent to which the perpetrator and his or her partner use violence in order to attempt to control the relationship. The four types constitute a typology of *individual* violence that is rooted in information about the couple and defined by the control context within which the violence is embedded (figure 1).

In *intimate terrorism*, the perpetrator uses violence in the service of general control over his or her partner; the partner does not. In *violent resistance*, the partner is violent and controlling—an intimate terrorist—and the resister's violence arises in reaction to that attempt to exert general control.[2] In *mutual violent control*, both members of the couple use violence in attempts to gain general control over their partner. Thus, three of the four types of intimate partner violence are organized around attempts to exert or thwart general control. In the fourth type of intimate partner violence, *situational couple violence*, the perpetrator is violent (and his or her partner may be as well); however, neither of them uses violence to attempt to exert general control.

The control that forms the basis of this typology of intimate partner violence and is the defining feature of intimate terrorism, is more than the specific,

Figure 1. Types of Domestic Violence

Intimate Terrorism
The individual is violent and controlling.
The partner is not.

Violent Resistance
It is the partner who is violent and controlling.
The individual is violent, but not controlling.

Situational Couple Violence
Although the individual is violent,
neither partner is both violent and controlling.

Mutual Violent Resistance
Both individual and partner are violent and controlling.

short-term control that is often the goal of violence in other contexts. The mugger wants to control you only briefly in order to take your valuables and move on, hopefully never to see you again. In contrast, the control sought in intimate terrorism is general and long term. Although each particular act of intimate violence may appear to have any number of short-term, specific goals, it is embedded in a larger pattern of power and control that permeates the relationship. This is the violence employed by the newlywed batterer quoted above, who sees his behavior as the embodiment of his "ownership" of his partner.

The core idea of this book is that this "intimate terrorism"—violence deployed in the service of general control over one's partner—is quite a different phenomenon than violence that is not motivated by an interest in exerting general control over one's partner. I would argue, also, that intimate terrorism is what most of us *mean* by "domestic violence." This is the violence that has received massive media attention, and that has been the focus of thirty years of feminist activism and research in the United States.

Intimate Terrorism and Other Types of Partner Violence

INTIMATE TERRORISM

Our discussion of the four types of partner violence begins with intimate terrorism because it involves the general exercise of coercive control that is the heart of the distinctions posed here. Figure 2 is a widely used graphical representation of partner violence deployed in the service of general control. This diagram and the understanding of domestic violence that lies behind it were developed over a period of years from the testimony of battered women in the Duluth, Minnesota, area, testimony that convinced the staff of the Duluth

Figure 2. The Power and Control Wheel

Source: Adapted from Ellen Pence and Michael Paymar, *Education Groups for Men Who Batter: The Duluth Model* (New York: Springer, 1993).

Domestic Abuse Intervention Project that the most important characteristic of the violence that they encountered was that it was embedded in a general pattern of power and control.[3] A *pattern* of power and control cannot, of course, be identified by looking at violence in isolation or by looking at one incident. It can only be recognized from information about the use of multiple control tactics over time, allowing one to find out whether a perpetrator uses more than one of these tactics to control his or her partner, indicating an attempt to exercise general control.

Let's work our way around the "spokes" of the diagram, clockwise, beginning with economic abuse at one o'clock. It is not unusual for an intimate terrorist to deprive his partner of control over economic resources.[4] He controls all the money. She is allowed no bank account and no credit cards. If she works for wages, she has to turn over her paychecks to him. He keeps all the cash and she has to ask him for money when she needs to buy groceries or clothes for herself or the children. He may require a precise accounting of every penny, demanding to see the grocery bill and making sure she returns every bit of the change. This economic abuse may be justified through the next form of control, male privilege: "I am the man of the house, the head of the household, the king in my castle." Of course, this use of male privilege can cover everything. As the man of the house, his word is law. He doesn't have to explain. She doesn't disagree with him. She is to do his bidding without question. And she doesn't talk back. All of this holds even more rigidly in public, where he is not to be humiliated by smart-talk from "his woman."

How does he use the children to support his control? First of all, they, too, know he is the boss. He makes it clear that he controls not only them, but their mother as well. He may use them to back him up, to make her humiliation more complete by forcing them into the room to assist him as he confronts her, asking them if he isn't right, and making them support his control of her. He may even have convinced them that he *should* be in charge, that he does know what is best (father knows best), and that she is incompetent or stupid or immoral. In addition, he may use her attachment to the children as a means of control, by threatening to take them away from her or hurt them if she isn't a "good wife and mother." Of course, being a good wife and mother means doing as he says.

Then there's isolation. Keep her away from everyone else. Make *himself* her only source of information, of support, of money, of everything. In a rural setting he might be able to literally isolate her, moving to a house trailer in the woods, with one car that he controls, no phone, keeping her there alone. In an urban setting, or if he needs her to go out to work, he can isolate her, though less literally, by driving away her friends and relatives and intimidating the people at work, so that she has no one to talk to about what's happening to her. When she's completely isolated, and what he tells her about herself is all she ever hears about herself, he can tell her over and over again that she's worthless, humiliate her, demean her, emotionally abuse her. She's ugly, stupid, a slut, a lousy wife, an incompetent mother. She only manages to survive because he takes care of her. She'd be helpless without him. And who else is there to tell her otherwise? Maybe he can convince her that she can't live without him.

Related to this emotional abuse is minimizing or denying his own abuse, and blaming her for what is going on in the relationship. It's her crazy behavior or incompetence or sexual misconduct that requires him to control her the way he does, in her own best interests. How could she see him as abusive? He's never really hurt her. On the contrary, she's the abusive partner. She's so out of touch with reality that maybe she should get some help.

If she resists, intimidate her. Show her what might happen if she doesn't behave. Scream at her. Swear at her. Let her see his rage. Smash things. Or maybe a little cold viciousness will make his point. Kick her cat. Hang her dog. That ought to make her think twice before she decides not to do as he says. Or threaten her. Threaten to hit her, or beat her, or pull her hair out, or burn her. Or tell her he'll kill her, maybe the kids, too.

Put all these means of control together, or even a few of them, and the abuser builds what Catherine Kirkwood calls a "web" of abuse.[5] He entraps and enslaves his partner. If she manages to thwart one means of control, there are others at his disposal. Wherever she turns, there is another way he can control her. Sometimes she is ensnared by multiple strands. She can't seem to escape—she is trapped. But with the addition of violence, there is more than entrapment. There is terror.

For this reason the diagram does not include the violence as just another means of control, another spoke in the wheel. The violence is depicted, rather, as the rim of the wheel, holding all the spokes together. When violence is added to such a pattern of power and control, the abuse becomes much more than the sum of its parts. The ostensibly nonviolent tactics that accompany that violence take on a new, powerful, and frightening meaning, controlling the victim not only through their own specific constraints, but also through their association with the general knowledge that her partner will do anything to maintain control of the relationship, even attack her physically. Most obviously, the threats and intimidation are something more than idle threats if he has beaten her before. But beyond that, his "request" to see the grocery receipts becomes a "warning" if he has put her into the hospital this year. His calling her a stupid slut may feel like the beginning of a vicious physical attack. As battered women often report, "All he had to do was look at me that way, and I'd jump." What is for most of us the safest place in our world, home, is for her a place of constant fear.

VIOLENT RESISTANCE

What is a woman to do when she finds herself terrorized in her own home?[6] At some point, most women in such relationships do fight back physically. For some, this is an instinctive reaction to being attacked, and it happens at the first blow—almost without thought. For others, it doesn't happen until it seems he is going to continue to assault her if she doesn't do something to stop him. For most women in heterosexual relationships, the size difference ensures that violent resistance won't help, and may make things worse, so they turn to other means of coping. For a few, eventually it seems that the only way out is to kill him.

The critical defining pattern of violent resistance is that the resister is violent but *not* controlling and is faced with a partner who is *both* violent and controlling; i.e., he is an intimate terrorist. Violence in the face of intimate terrorism may arise from any of a variety of motives. She may (at least at first) believe that she can defend herself, that her violent resistance will keep him from attacking her further. That may mean that she thinks she can stop him right now, in the midst of an attack, or it may mean that she thinks that if she fights back often enough he will eventually decide to stop attacking her physically. Even if she doesn't think she can stop him, she may feel that he shouldn't be allowed to attack her without getting hurt some himself. This desire to hurt him in return even if it won't stop him can be a form of communication ("What you're doing isn't right and I'm going to fight back as hard as I can"), or it may be a form of retaliation or payback, along the lines of "He's not going to do that without paying some price for it." In a few cases, she may be after serious retaliation, attacking him when he is least expecting it and doing her best to do serious damage, even killing him. But there is another, more frequent motive for such premeditated attacks—escape. Sometimes, after years of abuse and entrapment, a victim of intimate terrorism may feel that the only way she can escape from this horror is to kill her tormenter. Such cases have been the focus of some media attention, as in movies such as *The Burning Bed*,

Sleeping with the Enemy, and *Enough*. More importantly, the "battered woman defense" has achieved some credibility in the courts;[7] governors and parole boards have been considering clemency, pardons, or parole in cases in which the motive for the murder of an abusive partner was clearly to escape from a seemingly hopeless situation.[8]

SITUATIONAL COUPLE VIOLENCE

Probably the most common type of partner violence does not involve any attempt on the part of either partner to gain general control over the relationship. The violence is situationally provoked, as the tensions or emotions of a particular encounter lead someone to react with violence. Intimate relationships inevitably involve conflicts, and in some relationships one or more of those conflicts may escalate to violence. The violence may be minor and singular, with one argument at some point in the relationship escalating to the level that someone pushes or slaps the other, is immediately remorseful, apologizes, and never does it again. Or it could be a chronic problem, with one or both partners frequently resorting to violence, minor or severe. I don't want to minimize the danger of such violence. Situationally provoked violence can be life-threatening.

The motives for such violence vary. A physical reaction might feel like the only way one's extreme anger or frustration can be expressed. It may well be intended to do serious injury as an expression of anger. It may primarily be an attempt to get the attention of a partner who doesn't seem to be listening. Or there could be a control motive involved, albeit not one that is part of a general pattern of coercive control. One partner may simply find that the argument is not going well for him or her, and decide that one way to win this is to get physical.

The critical distinctions among types of violence have to do with general patterns of power and control, not with the ostensible motives for specific incidents of violence. Thus, many of the separate violent incidents of situational couple violence may look exactly like those involved in intimate terrorism or violent resistance. The difference is in the general power and control dynamic of the relationship, not in the nature of any one assault. If it appears that neither partner is generally trying to control the other—i.e., the relationship does not involve the use of a range of control tactics by one or both of the partners—then we are dealing with situational couple violence. It is simply that one or more disagreements have resulted in violence. The violence may even be frequent, if the situation that provokes the violence is recurring, as when one partner frequently feels that the other is flirting, and the confrontations over that issue regularly lead one or the other of them to lash out. And the violence may be quite severe, including even homicide. What makes it situational couple violence is that it is rooted in the events of a particular situation rather than in a relationshipwide attempt to control.

MUTUAL VIOLENT CONTROL

Finally, in a very small number of cases, both members of the couple are violent and controlling, each behaving in a manner that would identify him or her as an intimate terrorist if it weren't for the fact that their partner also seems to be engaged in the same sort of violent attempt to control the relationship. We know very little about the dynamics of such relationships other than that they seem to involve the "mutual combat" that researchers have for decades attributed to any relationship in which both partners reported that they had been violent. In most such cases, however, that so-called mutual violence was a product of intimate terrorism with violent resistance, or situational couple violence in which both partners had been violent. With mutual violent control, we have the true mutuality of two people fighting for general control over the relationship.

Doing Research on Intimate Terrorism and Other Types of Partner Violence

The descriptions of these four types of partner violence are derived from thirty years of social science research on violence between intimate partners, most of which does not distinguish among them. How, then, does one draw conclusions about these four different types of partner violence? The next three sections address this question. First, some of the more recent research does ask the right questions, inquiring about the violence and other control tactics that are used by both partners in a relationship. This section will briefly explain how researchers go about deciding which type of violence (if any) is involved in the relationships they study. The second section illustrates what is to be gained from such distinctions, by showing how they provide important insights into the differences between men's and women's perpetration of partner violence. However, given that these distinctions are relatively new to the research literature, there are hundreds (actually, probably thousands) of studies that report on partner violence but do not ask the right questions. Do not despair. Many of those studies can be used to give us some insight into the differences among the major types of partner violence. The third section addresses the "tricks" that I have used to tease as much information as possible out of the "old style" research that didn't make distinctions among types of domestic violence.

ASKING THE RIGHT QUESTIONS:
THE NATURE OF COERCIVE CONTROL

Coercive control is the key to understanding the differences among the basic types of partner violence. Once we know that someone has been violent toward his or her partner, the next thing we need to know is whether that violence was enacted in a general context of power and control—and we need similar information about the partner.[9] The challenge to researchers, then, is to ask the questions that will allow our respondents to tell us the extent to which they or their partners are doing what they believe has to be done in order to gain overall control.

How do we know coercive control when we see it? The core measurement idea is rather simple: if a violent individual is known to use a wide variety of tactics to control his or her partner, then it is reasonable to assume that the violence itself is being enacted in the service of that control, and we are dealing with a case of coercive control.[10] One of the great difficulties confronted in the study of violence is identifying the motives behind any particular violent act or encounter. Violence is not always motivated by a desire to gain or resist control.[11] Sometimes it is primarily an expression of anger or frustration. Sometimes it is a matter of self-image. Sometimes it is simply a bid for attention. It is not easy to know in any specific encounter what the real motives of the perpetrator might be. In the case of partner violence, however, we don't need to settle for information about one act or one encounter. With partner violence we are looking not at an isolated encounter between two people (such as a mugging or a bar fight), but at a close relationship, a pattern of encounters that extends over a period of time and involves a variety of situations.[12] We can place the individual's violence in the general context of that relationship. Thus, we ask questions about the general use of control tactics throughout the relationship.

The primary source of ideas about exactly which questions to ask is women who have been victims of battering and abuse by their partners.[13] What they have been telling us for decades is that the violence is not all of it, or in some cases not even the worst of it.[14] These reports from women have been used over the years by researchers in sociology, psychology, criminology, and other disciplines to develop a wide variety of questions, questionnaires, and scales that have been used in research, but this work was usually framed as the study of emotional or psychological *abuse*. What feminist researchers recognized early on in this research was that the behavior being studied was not merely a collection of mindlessly abusive acts, but a set of tactics used by batterers to take control of their partners. Although these research measures did include questions about the kind of humiliating and demeaning verbal attacks that we typically associate with psychological abuse, they also included a wide range of controlling tactics that were simply coercive. It is important that we see these behaviors for what they are.

Feminist researchers have long recognized that the common element in these patterns is coercion—the exercise of power and imposition of control over your partner. Rebecca and Russell Dobash saw the pattern as rooted in patriarchal traditions of male domination in marriage.[15] Diana Russell, studying marital rape, recognized the similarity between the tactics used by batterers and Biderman's Chart of Coercion, developed in his studies of the brainwashing of U.S. prisoners of war during the Korean War.[16] The centrality of matters of power and control was captured graphically in Ellen Pence and Michael Paymar's Power and Control Wheel (see figure 2).[17] Current work in this area, especially that by Mary Ann Dutton and Lisa Goodman and by Evan Stark, is moving away from merely listing the abusive or controlling behaviors of batterers to a more theoretical approach focused on the concept of coercive control.[18]

Coercion involves getting someone to do something they do not want to do by "using or threatening . . . negative consequences for noncompliance."[19] An analysis of the essential process of coercive control reveals that it involves most of the tactics commonly identified by battered women as features of their batterers' behaviors. First, there is the violence itself, which is contingent violence; i.e., violence enacted as punishment for a failure to comply with the explicit or implicit demands of the intimate terrorist. As I noted above, any particular violent incident may not involve a clear component of control. The violent partner might say that he or she simply "lost it," that the violence was not a calculated act; intimate terrorists often see their behavior not as calculating and controlling, but as "out of control."[20] Or the attack may seem to come out of nowhere, as in cases in which women awake from a sound sleep to find themselves being beaten. In order to determine whether the violence is in fact part of a pattern of intimate terrorism, we have to ask if other elements of coercive control are present in the relationship.

Dutton and Goodman point out that effective coercive control requires a second element: the perpetrator must make it clear that he or she is willing and able to impose punishment if "necessary." This is where the threats and intimidation that are often reported by battered women come in. Such threats as "If you try to leave me, I'll kill you and the children" make clear the contingency and willingness to punish: "If you stay, nothing will happen; if you don't, you'll pay for it." Or the children might be used in another way, in threats to take custody of them if the partner leaves. Targets of intimate terrorism often report that one of the reasons they don't leave such relationships sooner is that they are afraid that their partner might actually be able to take their children away from them. Illegal immigrants may feel especially vulnerable to such threats.[21] Intimidation, through the destruction of property or through attacks on pets, makes it clear that the intimate terrorist is not only willing but able to use violence. A damaged wall or destroyed piece of furniture demonstrates the physical ability to do serious damage. The intimate terrorist husband whose wife comes home "late" and is given a lesson by being sent out to the garage to find the body of her dog has learned that her partner is vicious enough to kill.

Dutton and Goodman also point out that coercive control requires surveillance. In order to punish for "misbehavior," the intimate terrorist has to monitor his or her partner's behavior. The literature on domestic violence is full of examples of partners who require full reports of the day's activities, who make frequent phone calls to make sure their partner is where she is "supposed to be," who have friends spying on their partner, or who do their own snooping to uncover evidence of behavior that "requires correction."

A fourth basic element of coercive control is wearing down the partner's resistance. Intimate terrorists use a variety of tactics to undermine their partner's willingness or ability to fight for freedom from control. With respect to the will to resist, the actual violence and the threats and intimidation can induce a terror that keeps partners from daring to call their life their own. But intimate terrorists also use more subtle techniques, many of which involve the forms of emotional and psychological abuse that have been the focus of so much research in psychology and social work.[22] Intimate terrorists work to convince their partners that the latter are lazy, incompetent, stupid, oversexed, sexually frigid, bad parents, poor wives—in a word, worthless. An individual who feels worthless does not have the will to resist. A related tactic for reducing the will to resist is legitimation: convincing the partner that the intimate terrorist has the right to control and punish. Legitimation may take the form of an assertion of status as head of household. Or it might be closely tied up with the psychological attacks on self-esteem just discussed above, as in, "You are so incompetent and useless that I have to take control." This tactic may then lead to blaming the violence on her—if only she could do her job, or behave herself, or understand his needs, etc., then he wouldn't drink, lose control, have to punish her, or whatever his excuses are for the use of violence.

With regard to the ability to resist, intimate terrorists do what they can to cut their partner off from the resources required for effective resistance. As discussed above, one important resource is money. Employability can be controlled by refusing to allow continuing education, by harassment on the job, or by undermining job performance with late-night fights or sudden un-availability for promised childcare.[23] Paychecks, welfare payments, child support, and other income may be confiscated. The partner may be given a strict allowance, barely enough to meet the everyday shopping needs for the family. Another important resource for resistance is social support, and intimate terrorists isolate their partners. As we have seen, sometimes the isolation is physical, accomplished by moving away from friends and family, or eliminating all means of communication with the outside world. In other cases the isolation is accomplished psychologically, by harassing friends and family until they avoid all contact, and by undermining employment or education that might provide opportunities to talk with others.

You'll see that in discussing these elements of coercive control, we have covered the Power and Control Wheel. What this means is that we now have a theoretical understanding of the pattern of behaviors that battered women have told us characterize their partners' behaviors. Anyone who is serious about using violence to control their partner has to engage in enough of these behaviors to make their attempts to coerce effective. Thus we can use questions about threats, intimidation, surveillance, and reducing resistance to identify a pattern of coercive, controlling violence and to distinguish it from violence that is not being enacted in the service of control, inferring that violent partners who engage in more than a few of these behaviors are using violence in the service of control. That is exactly the approach that my colleagues and I use in our research on partner violence. First, we put together a series of questions about the elements of coercive control and created a coercive control score. Next, we distinguished those who had high coercive control scores from those who did not. We then used this distinction to separate the violent partners into two groups, a controlling violent group and a non-controlling violent group. Finally, we added similar information about their partners to determine whether their violence was intimate terrorism, violent resistance, situational couple violence, or mutual violent control.

This set of distinctions is essential to even the most minimal understanding of what goes on when someone physically attacks his or her intimate partner. Intimate partner violence enacted to establish and maintain general control over one's partner is very different from the other forms of violence in intimate relationships, and this long-unrecognized difference has been the source of much confusion and conflict in the research literature on intimate partner violence. Probably the most important example of this confusion and conflict is a longstanding and extremely acrimonious debate about women's involvement in partner violence. The angry scholarly debate has bled over into the media, as the entertainment appeal of the idea of a "battered husband" or "girls who beat up their boyfriends" has turned the issue into "news." The next section shows how the simple recognition that there are different types of partner violence can make sense of apparently contradictory research findings regarding this central disagreement among the experts.

NOT ASKING THE RIGHT QUESTIONS: THE BATTERED HUSBAND FIASCO

In 1977, in one of the first publications to come out of the groundbreaking 1975 National Family Violence Survey, Suzanne Steinmetz ignited a decades-long and not-yet-dead debate about the nature of partner violence. Her article, "The Battered Husband Syndrome," argued that there were as many battered husbands in U.S. families as there were battered wives.[24] Her article was immediately answered with intense criticism, a great scholarly debate ensued, and over the years hundreds of studies have addressed the issue of gender symmetry in partner violence.[25] While we have amassed a great deal of scientific evidence that men are far and away more likely than women to be perpetrators of domestic violence,[26] there also appears to be considerable evidence that women are just as likely as men to attack their partners.[27] The debate on this issue has been so acrimonious that, in the late 1990s, I was unable to persuade the protagonists to take part in a panel discussion of the issue at scholarly meetings, the parties basically refusing to be in the same room with each other. How did we come to have two groups of renowned scholars presenting ostensibly credible evidence for their obviously contradictory positions regarding the simplest possible question about partner violence: "Who does it?"?

The answer is that a terrible mistake characterized research on partner violence from the beginning of its development in the early 1970s. No one was thinking about distinguishing among types of partner violence. Researchers assumed that "violence was violence," that although there might be differences in how often and how severely partners assaulted each other, intimate partner violence was essentially one phenomenon. There were two major groups of social scientists doing this early research, but doing it from quite different perspectives and using different sources of data.[28] The "family violence scholars" were interested in violence between parents and their children and between siblings, as well as violence between spouses. Violence was seen as an outcome of family conflict. They did large-scale surveys, interviewing large numbers of U.S. husbands and wives, and were distressed to find that family conflict led many spouses, siblings, and parents to assault other family members in the privacy of their own homes.[29] The "feminist scholars" were focused more specifically on wife abuse. They studied agency data from the police, courts, emergency rooms, and shelters, and they interviewed women who had come to these agencies for help. Violence was seen as a product of patriarchal family traditions and general male dominance in the society. They were appalled at the number of women who were terrorized in their own homes.[30] The two groups of scholars did, however, have at least one thing in common: they each thought that their own research identified the true nature of partner violence. They have been at an impasse over the gender issue for almost thirty years.

The simple solution to this dilemma (simple once you see it) is that the two groups are studying different kinds of partner violence.[31] How can this be? In general, the studies that demonstrate the predominance of male violence involve agency data (courts, police agencies, hospitals, and shelters), while the studies that show gender symmetry involve the "representative" samples of large-scale survey research. Both of these research strategies are heavily biased, the former through its use of biased sampling frames (agency client lists), the latter through refusals. Although the biases of agency data are generally taken to be obvious,[32] representative sample surveys are mistakenly assumed to be unbiased. In fact, the final samples of so-called random sample surveys are *not* random—due to refusals. I have estimated, for example, that the refusal rate in the National Family Violence Surveys was approximately 40 percent rather than the 18 percent usually reported.[33] Could there be two qualitatively different forms of partner violence, one gender-symmetric and overrepresented in general surveys, the other male-perpetrated and overrepresented in agency samples?

In my early work (1995) on this question, I identified a number of agency-based studies and general surveys that used the same set of questions to assess the nature of partner violence.[34] My conclusion from comparing these findings was that the two sampling strategies identify partner violence that differs not only in gender symmetry, but also in a variety of other important ways. Agency samples identify partner violence that is more frequent, more likely to escalate, more severe, less likely to be mutual, and perpetrated almost entirely by men. This gender-asymmetric pattern resonated for me with feminist analyses of partner violence as one tactic in a general pattern of controlling behaviors used by some men to exercise general control over "their" women.[35] The asymmetry of such control contrasted dramatically, it seemed to me, with the family violence perspective's predominantly symmetric image of partner violence as a matter of conflict. I hypothesized that there were two qualitatively different forms/patterns of partner violence—one part of a general strategy of power and control (intimate terrorism), the other involving violence that is not part of a general pattern of control, probably a product of the escalation of couple conflict into violence (situational couple violence).[36] I argued that each research group was unknowingly studying only one of these two types of violence. Couples involved in situational couple violence are unlikely to become agency clients, because such situationally provoked violence does not, in most cases, call for police intervention, emergency room visits, Protection from Abuse orders, an escape to a shelter, or a divorce. Couples involved in intimate terrorism are unlikely to agree to participate in general surveys—the victims out of fear of reprisal from the batterer, the batterers out of fear of exposing themselves to intervention by the police or other agencies. Although these arguments seemed reasonable enough, my 1995 paper provides no direct evidence of their validity because, at that time, no one had made such distinctions among types of violence.

Here is the evidence. The data come from a unique study designed by Irene Frieze in the 1970s. The women she interviewed came from a variety of sources, including agencies (courts and shelters) and a general sample. Thus, if my theory was correct, her sample was likely to include both situational couple violence and intimate terrorism (and its response, violent resistance). One source of respondents was a flyer placed in laundromats. The second source was a shelter sample of women who had sought help at one of the Pittsburgh area shelters for battered women. Another group consisted of women who had filed for a Protection from Abuse order (PFA) in the courts. The fourth source was women who lived on the same block as the women in each of the first three groups; i.e., this group had not been selected because of violence and, therefore, probably was quite similar to the typical general survey sample.

From the lengthy interview protocols, I chose one question to determine whether the husband and/or wife had been violent, as reported by the wife: "Has he (Have you) ever actually slapped or pushed you (him) or used other physical force with you (him)?" I also selected eleven questions tapping control tactics that did not involve violence toward one's partner. From them, I constructed a coercive control scale and split it into a high-control group and a low-control group. The information regarding the violence and control of both partners was then used to designate each spouse as either nonviolent or involved in one of the four types of partner violence.[37] Given my initial interest in the gender debate, my first question was whether the Pittsburgh data supported my idea that (a) the violence in general survey samples consists mostly of situational couple violence, while the violence in agency samples is mostly intimate terrorism and violent resistance, and (b) situational couple violence is gender-symmetric, intimate terrorism is mostly male-perpetrated, with violent resistors therefore mostly women.

First, let's nail down the sampling argument. Do general survey samples tap primarily situational couple violence, while agency samples give access primarily to intimate terrorism (and violent resistance)? Looking first at male violence, table 1 shows that in the Pittsburgh study's general sample (a type of sample that is typical of family violence research), the violent men are involved mostly in situational couple violence, with only 11 percent of their violence being intimate terrorism. In the agency samples, intimate terrorism is much more typical, representing 46 percent of the men's violence in the court data

TABLE 1. Men's Violence in Different Samples

	Survey sample (n = 37)	Court sample (n = 35)	Shelter sample (n = 50)
Mutual violent control	0%	11%	2%
Intimate terrorism	11%	46%	66%
Violent resistance	3%	6%	4%
Situational couple violence	86%	37%	28%

TABLE 2 . Women's Violence in Different Samples

	Survey sample (n = 29)	Court sample (n = 29)	Shelter sample (n = 38)
Mutual violent control	0%	14%	3%
Intimate terrorism	3%	7%	5%
Violent resistance	10%	**41%**	**61%**
Situational couple violence	**86%**	31%	32%

and 66 percent in the shelter data. Table 2 presents the data regarding women's violence, which are the other side of the same picture. Situational couple violence dominates the women's violence in the survey sample, while violent resistance is the largest category in the shelter sample, with the court data being intermediate.

Before we move on, let's think about this for a moment. The results for the general sample are much as predicted: targets of intimate terrorism are evidently not willing to participate in general surveys, and we can reasonably assume that any findings from general surveys apply to situational couple violence, not to intimate terrorism. The data from the courts and the shelter, however, surprised me. I had expected agency data to be heavily dominated by men's intimate terrorism and women's violent resistance, but there are considerably more cases of situational couple violence than I had thought there would be. Where did I go wrong? I had mistakenly assumed that only intimate terrorism would frighten women enough to send them to the courts for a Protection from Abuse order, or to a shelter for support or temporary housing. I hadn't paid close enough attention to my own statements that even situational couple violence can be quite frequent and/or severe. And I hadn't taken seriously enough the evidence from general surveys (thus dealing with situational couple violence) that men's situational couple violence is much more likely than women's to produce injuries.[38] Shelters and courts are places that women turn to when they fear for their safety. Although intimate terrorism is certainly the type of violence that is most likely to produce such a reaction, situational couple violence involving a man assaulting a woman can also be severe enough or frequent enough to be quite frightening. Thus, although the relatively large

TABLE 3. Gender Symmetry of Types of Violence

	Husbands	Wives	(n)
Intimate terrorism	89%	11%	(81)
Violent resistance	15%	85%	(61)
Situational couple violence	55%	45%	(167)
Mutual violent control*	50%	50%	(16)

*Mutual violent control is symmetrical by definition in heterosexual relationships.

number of cases of situational couple violence in the shelter and court samples was somewhat surprising, in retrospect the pattern makes sense.[39] General samples involve almost entirely cases of situational couple violence, while agency samples involve a mix of intimate terrorism and the most frightening cases of situational couple violence.[40]

The data in tables 1 and 2 establish that the different sampling strategies do, indeed, tap different kinds of violence. Are the gender differences in violence type such that those biases could have created the gender debate? The answer clearly is "Yes," as you can see from table 3. Eighty-nine percent of the intimate terrorists in the Pittsburgh data were men.[41] Of course, it follows that in this sample of heterosexual couples almost all of the violent resistance comes from women (85 percent). In dramatic contrast to the clear gendering of intimate terrorism and violent resistance is situational couple violence, which is close to gender-symmetric, at least by the crude criterion of prevalence (data on the frequency and consequences of men's and women's situational couple violence, shown in chapter 4, indicate that by other criteria men are more violent than women, even within situational couple violence). Mutual violent control, which is very rare, is gender-symmetric by definition in heterosexual couples, because it is defined by both partners' being violent and controlling.[42]

That explains the gender fiasco, doesn't it? Men and women are equally involved only in situational couple violence.[43] When someone goes on television or publishes a paper to pronounce that the survey evidence proves that women are as violent as men in intimate relationships, they are suggesting that women are as likely as men to be batterers and abusers—intimate terrorists. And the suggestion is not subtle. They tell stories about some of the few women who are, indeed, intimate terrorists,[44] or they are on a talk show in which the panel consists of "girls who beat up their boyfriends" or "men who are afraid of their wives." But we have just shown that *survey* data about violence are only about situational couple violence, not intimate terrorism. Intimate terrorism is in fact perpetrated almost entirely by men.

And situational couple violence isn't anything like intimate terrorism. Here are some data about the violence perpetrated by the men from the Pittsburgh study. The violence in men's intimate terrorism is quite frequent; the modal number of incidents in these marriages is one hundred![45] The modal number of violent events in men's situational couple violence is one. Intimate terrorism escalated in severity of violence in 72 percent of the cases; situational couple violence escalated in only 29 percent. In terms of injuries, the violence of intimate terrorism was severe in 67 percent of the cases, compared to 29 percent of the cases of situational couple violence. These data do not leave much doubt that intimate terrorism and situational couple violence are not the same phenomenon.[46] We need to make these distinctions.

WHEN THE RIGHT QUESTIONS AREN'T ASKED, WHERE DO WE FIND THE TYPES?

This book reviews the research literature on the nature of these types of partner violence and on their causes and consequences. There are a few recent studies that explicitly make the distinctions, but most of the literature I review does not. How can we make use of thirty years of research on partner violence in spite of this deficiency? First, we start our thinking about each question with the few studies that do make the distinctions. Then, we "tweak" the other research to see if it supports our conclusions.

There are two pretty useful clues to be used in the interpretation of the old data. One is the sampling biases noted above. The violence in general survey research is almost entirely men's and women's situational couple violence. Thus, any survey research that compares violent with nonviolent men or women—or victims with nonvictims—can be reliably assumed to tell us about situational couple violence. In contrast, the violence in agency samples is almost all men's intimate terrorism and women's violent resistance. Thus, agency-based studies can be used to inform us regarding those two types of violence. That leaves mutual violent control as our only mystery. Unfortunately, it will have to remain a mystery for now. The few studies that do distinguish among types of domestic violence have found very few cases that appear to involve mutual violent control. This means both that we have too few to give us any sense of the nature of this phenomenon and that, whatever its dynamic, it is very rare. For now, we will have to focus on the three major types of domestic violence: intimate terrorism, violent resistance, and situational couple violence.

The second trick we can use with the old literature is to look for patterns associated with each of the three major types of violence. For example, violence that is frequent and severe is most likely to be intimate terrorism. Violence that is infrequent and mild is more likely to be situational couple violence. Thus, if studies show that anger management therapy is only effective in the treatment of men whose violence is infrequent and mild, we have indirect support for the conclusion that it is effective for situational couple violence but not effective for intimate terrorism. We'll need to be very careful with this tactic because, as I pointed out above, although infrequent and mild violence is likely to be situational couple violence, some of it is, in fact, intimate terrorism. So, this second tweaking tactic will be used only to back up conclusions that already have support from our two major sources of information—studies that make the distinctions and studies that use samples whose biases pretty much tell us what kind of violence they are studying.

The following chapters look at each of the three major types of partner violence. What are their societal, interpersonal and individual causes? How do they develop in a relationship and what do they look like? What are their effects on their victims? How do victims try to stop them, cope with them, or escape from them? How effective are various interventions, such as arrest and incarceration and various forms of counseling? What sorts of public policies and legislation are likely to be most effective in stopping them or mitigating their effects? Until now, answers to these questions have been based on the misleading lumping together of all partner violence under the label of "domestic violence." We know that this error has produced some important but obvious contradictions, such as the battered-husband fiasco that continues today. There are probably a great many, more-hidden errors. Once we take into account the differences among intimate terrorism, violent resistance, and situational couple violence, we will have a much clearer picture of what is going on in violent families.

Intimate
Terrorism
Controlling
Your
Partner

Thanks to the second wave of the women's movement, we actually know a good deal about intimate terrorism, more than we know about
the other forms of domestic violence. Because one of the major successes of
the women's movement has been to draw attention to the problem of wife
beating, we have the benefit of thirty years of feminist research on men's use
of violence to control their partners.[1] Most of this body of feminist research on
domestic violence is based on interviews with women who were contacted
through hospitals, the courts, and shelters; as I have shown in chapter 1, the
women who come into contact with those agencies are much more likely to be
experiencing intimate terrorism than any other type of partner violence. Thus,
although this research did not make explicit distinctions among types of violence, it is reasonable to assume that the major patterns identified are those
associated with intimate terrorism. Furthermore, in many cases we can do
more than merely assume that the violence is intimate terrorism, because one
of the major strengths of this research is that it involves a healthy mix of quantitative and qualitative analyses. Feminist researchers have not been afraid to
ask women to tell their stories, which are dominated by accounts of men's use
of violence to take general control over "their" women.

Intimate terrorism does appear in the same-sex relationships of both men
and women; moreover, there are unquestionably some women who do terrorize their male partners. However, because intimate terrorism is perpetrated in
large part by men against their women partners, and because we know so little
about the intimate terrorism of lesbians, gay men, and heterosexual women,
I focus this chapter on men's intimate terrorism in heterosexual relationships,
and my choice of pronouns reflects that focus.

The Basic Characteristics of (Heterosexual Men's) Intimate Terrorism

Let's begin with a look at the basic characteristics of intimate terrorism. By "basic" characteristics I mean the characteristics that *define* intimate terrorism. An intimate terrorist is violent and highly controlling—by *definition*. Intimate terrorism is about violent, coercive control. The intimate terrorist uses physical violence in combination with a variety of other control tactics to exercise general, coercive control over his partner.[2] This powerful combination of violence with a general pattern of control is terrorizing because once a controlling partner has been violent, all of his other controlling actions take on the threat of violence. A look, a yell, a quiet warning, even an ostensibly benign request can have the emotional impact of a physical assault. Catherine Kirkwood describes it like this: "The women's descriptions of waiting for an attack, wondering about the intensity, searching their experience and resources for any method of diffusing the potential violence, all constitute a type of mental and emotional torture, and in fact their partners' behavior has been likened to the behaviour of captors who emotionally torture prisoners of war. . . ."[3] Let's look first at the nonviolent control tactics, then at the typical pattern of violence in intimate terrorism.[4]

NONVIOLENT CONTROL TACTICS

Threats and Intimidation. Intimate terrorists often "lay down the law" through threats and intimidation. One of the questions asked of the wives in the Pittsburgh study was "Has your husband ever gotten angry and *threatened* to use physical force with you?" Ninety-seven percent of the wives experiencing intimate terrorism had been threatened; 61 percent, "often."[5] They were also asked about intimidation, which doesn't involve a direct threat but, rather, a display of the capacity to do damage. Thus, an intimate terrorist may express his *anger with his wife* by directing it toward objects (92 percent in this study) or toward the children or pets (65 percent). One of the more gut-wrenching cases of intimidation at the shelter where I work involves a woman who told a colleague of mine that one day when she didn't arrive home "on time," her husband told her to go look out in the garage—where she found that he had hanged her dog.

Sometimes the rules that the woman must follow in order to avoid punishment are quite clear. For example, one of Dobash and Dobash's informants in Scotland told them, "We were two miles from the village. He allowed me half an hour to go up to the village and half an hour to walk back and ten minutes to get what I needed in the shops. That was what I was allowed, an hour and ten minutes. If I [wasn't] back inside that hour and ten minutes I got met at the door saying where the f——ing hell have you been."[6] In other cases the "rules" are so vague that partners who wish to comply in order to avoid punishment face a nearly impossible task in figuring out what will and what won't get them attacked: "He'd say, you made me hit you, you know. And I didn't realize what I was doing to make him hit me, but he did say it."[7]

Monitoring. The violence and threats and intimidation may get the message across that the intimate terrorist will "do what he has to do" in order to have his way, but he can't exact punishment if he doesn't know about transgressions. Thus, in order to maintain control, intimate terrorists may monitor their partner's behavior closely. Three-fifths of the intimate terrorists in the Pittsburgh data *always* knew where their wife was when they weren't together; 96 percent always or usually knew.

Undermining the Will to Resist. Intimate terrorists undermine their partner's will to resist with beatings and other punishment in reaction to any real or imagined resistance, and with constant psychological attacks designed to destroy her self-confidence and convince her that she has no viable alternatives to this relationship. Pittsburgh data on the violence of intimate terrorism (below, in this chapter) shows that it is generally (although not always) frequent, severe, and unilateral. As for psychological control and abuse, although there were no questions regarding this tactic in the Pittsburgh interviews, the general pattern of findings in the research literature is quite clear; reports based on agency data are full of detailed accounts of relentless psychological abuse.

> ". . . and he would go 'ssss' . . . like he was letting air out of the top of my head [like I was an airhead]. And he would do it about real little things to my views on world issues."[8]

> ". . . name-calling. And picking fault in my appearance. Or even pathetic things like picking fault in the way my underarms smelt, just really ridiculous childish things. . . . Just a part of the pattern of things."[9]

The will to resist is also undermined by justifications of the violence that shift the blame to her or that legitimate the violence in terms of his role as head of the household.

"He maintained he was in the right: I deserved the black eye. So, therefore, to me, he wasn't ashamed of it. I felt about the size of twopence. I felt terribly embarrassed at this black eye and what was inside me."[10]

"I think the pattern that was established early and continued on was, 'Okay, figure out what's going on here and adjust to it. Adjust yourself, adjust what you're doing, and then things might quiet down.'"[11]

In some cases this constant abuse can leave a woman feeling completely inadequate or even uncertain as to who she is, what she believes, or what is real and what is not.

"My self-esteem and self-worth and everything just plummeted. I just kept trying to be what he wanted me to be."[12]

"You don't have any reality base. Cause what you see is not what you're told is happening, *constantly*. It's like that whole thing with that jealousy when I *knew* I wasn't doing anything. And yet, after a while I would [think] where there's smoke there's fire—what am I doing? I must be doing something."[13]

"I was sinking into a surreal existence."[14]

Undermining the Ability to Resist. Because many women, nevertheless, do continue to resist control, intimate terrorists also work to restrict access to the resources needed for effective resistance. An intimate terrorist may not allow his partner to work, or, if she does, she may have to hand over every paycheck, from which he gives her just enough "allowance" to cover household expenses. And she may be required to account for every penny. The women in Pittsburgh were asked how much money they had to spend in an average week without accounting to anyone. The average amount of money a woman was allowed to control weekly was $38 for women in nonviolent relationships and $41 for those experiencing situational couple violence, but only $19 for those experiencing intimate terrorism (all amounts are in 1970 dollars).[15] Fully 30 percent of the women experiencing intimate terrorism had no money at all to spend at their own discretion.

One of the most important resources is other people—people who might help the partner understand what is happening to her, encourage her to resist or leave, or even offer financial and logistical support.

"People weren't allowed to call me at all. *Nobody* could call me
ever. . . . and he said 'you don't have time for friends! The only things
you have time to do are study and take care of *me*. . . .'"[16]

All of these nonviolent tactics of control undermine her will to resist and/or
her ability to resist, and help the intimate terrorist to maintain control. Of
course, all of these tactics function within the context of violence; violence
that for many intimate terrorists is frequent and severe.

THE NATURE AND PATTERN OF THE VIOLENCE

Although intimate terrorism is not defined by the frequency or severity of
the violence involved, the data clearly indicate that such violence is more likely
than the violence in situational couple violence to escalate and to be frequent
and severe.[17] In the Pittsburgh data, the average number of violent incidents is
ten per year of marriage, as compared with two per year for cases of situational
couple violence. In 72 percent of the cases the intimate terrorist became more
violent over time.[18] Over two-thirds (67 percent) of the women experiencing
intimate terrorism had been severely injured in the most serious incident of
violence.[19]

It is tempting simply to characterize intimate terrorism as involving frequent and severe violence. The attempt to exert general control, when combined with the resistance that is to be anticipated in a culture in which the vast
majority of women expect an egalitarian relationship, often leads intimate terrorists to resort to frequent and/or severe violence. However, a look at the variability in the nature of the violence reminds us that intimate terrorist violence
is *not necessarily* frequent or severe. In the Pittsburgh data, thirty-three percent
of the women experiencing intimate terrorism had never been severely injured; in fact, 12 percent of them had never been injured at all. Similarly, with
respect to frequency, nineteen of these eighty-eight women (22 percent) had
been physically attacked less often than once a year.

What about the issue of mutuality? As discussed in chapter 1, one of the
great debates in the domestic violence research literature has concerned so-
called mutual combat, with some scholars arguing that most domestic violence
is mutual. Again, many of the generalizations debated within this research literature have been "resolved" on the basis of studies in which no distinctions
were made among the types of violence; once more, we will see that the truth
depends on which type of violence you're talking about. The Pittsburgh data
allow me to address the question of mutuality in a number of ways.

First, only 25 percent of the women experiencing intimate terrorism had *never* been violent toward their partner. Thus, by the standard criterion used for mutuality, 75 percent of the cases of intimate terrorism did involve "mutual" violence. Second, however, looking only at intimate terrorists whose partners *had* been violent, the intimate terrorists themselves had been violent in thirty-six more incidents on average than had their partners. (The comparable figure for situational couple violence is eight.) Looked at another way, on average, male intimate terrorists are violent thirteen times more frequently than their "mutually violent" partners. Third, defining mutuality in terms of injuries, only 14 percent of these men had ever experienced a severe injury as a result of their partner's violence; as noted above, in this section, 67 percent of them had severely injured their partners. Fourth, while many of the partners of intimate terrorists may have resisted with violence early on, most of them had stopped by the time of the interview. Seventy-one percent had not been violent in the past six months. Looking at it another way, the women who had responded to intimate terrorism with violence had stopped their violence on average twenty-two months before their partners' most recent attack. (For mutual situational couple violence, men had stopped being violent two months earlier than their partners.)

Thus, while it is true that by the simplistic but commonly-used criterion of both partners having been violent at least once in their relationship, 75 percent of these cases of intimate terrorism involve mutual violence, the rest of the data make it clear how ridiculous that standard criterion for mutuality is. Among these so-called mutually violent couples, the men are violent thirteen times more often than their wives and are five times more likely to inflict a severe injury, and the women who do at first respond with violence desist on average nearly two years before the men's violence ends.

Summing up, we can say that (a) there is considerable variability in the violence involved in intimate terrorism, and (b) on average, male intimate terrorists are frighteningly violent. The average frequency of violent incidents is almost one per month, 67 percent of these men have seriously injured their partners, and, by any reasonable criterion of mutuality, the violence involved in these relationships is far from mutual.

Who Are the Intimate Terrorists?

Remember, first, that intimate terrorists are mostly men—that is why this chapter focuses on men—and we do know something about who they are.[20] Recent research on the types of men who assault their intimate partners not only supports my distinction between the two most frequent types of men's domestic violence (intimate terrorism and situational couple violence), but also provides a convergence of findings that indicates that there are two quite different types of intimate terrorists.

TWO TYPES OF INTIMATE TERRORISTS: PSYCHOLOGICAL COMMONALITIES AND DIFFERENCES

Amy Holtzworth-Munroe and her colleagues have been involved in an extensive program of research that clearly identifies two different types of intimate terrorists. They began with a careful review of previous studies that had made distinctions among types of so-called batterers, and they concluded that it appeared that there were three types.[21] They then carried out a series of studies that confirmed those conclusions, using a statistical technique that identified clusters of batterers who had similar profiles with respect to a number of personality and psychological traits, severity of the marital violence, and involvement in violence toward people outside of the marriage.[22] They found one type that clearly corresponds to situational couple violence, and two that are subtypes of intimate terrorists.[23] I will refer to the three as actors in situational couple violence, dependent intimate terrorists, and antisocial intimate terrorists. The actors in situational couple violence are, on average, involved in relatively low-level violence, are not violent outside of the family, exhibit the same psychological profiles as those of men in nonviolent control groups, and resemble nonviolent men in most respects. We'll come back to them in a later chapter.

Let's begin the discussion of the two remaining types with what they have in common. First, they clearly are intimate terrorists. Both (dependent intimate terrorists and antisocial intimate terrorists) are involved in relatively high levels of marital violence and in broad patterns of controlling behavior.[24] In terms of personality and attitudes, both of these types of intimate terrorists are impulsive and accepting of violence. Both are also hostile toward women.

It is important that I take a moment here to discuss the research on the relationship between domestic violence and attitudes toward women. I considered putting this digression into an endnote, as I often do with supporting research, but this issue is especially important because critics of feminist theory often claim that there is no relationship between attitudes toward women and domestic violence.[25] Such claims notwithstanding, the studies addressing this question do clearly support the position that individual men's attitudes toward women affect the likelihood that they will be involved in domestic violence. One example is Holtzworth-Munroe's work, cited above, showing that her two intimate terrorist clusters are more hostile toward women than are either nonviolent men or men involved in situational couple violence. More generally, in 1996 Sugarman and Frankel conducted a thorough review of the research on this question, using a statistical technique that allowed them to combine the findings of all of the studies published up to that time. While Holtzworth-Munroe demonstrated an effect of *hostility toward women*, Sugarman and Frankel focused on the effects of men's *attitudes concerning the role of women* in social life; they found that traditional men were more likely to be involved in attacks on their partners than were nontraditional men.[26]

The details of the Sugarman and Frankel review provide further support for the important role of attitudes toward women in intimate terrorism. They found that men's attitudes toward women were much more strongly related to violence in studies using samples dominated by intimate terrorism than in studies dominated by situational couple violence.[27] Of course, this is exactly what the feminist theory of domestic violence would predict. It is intimate terrorism that involves the attempt to control one's partner, an undertaking supported by traditional attitudes toward women.

The general picture of intimate terrorists, then, is that they are men who are generally accepting of violence, impulsive, hostile toward women, and traditional in their sex role attitudes. It is perhaps easy to see how acceptance of violence, impulsivity, and negative or even traditional attitudes toward women might lead to violence toward women, but it is the other ways that these men differ from the men involved in situational couple violence and from each other that give us clues as to the psychological roots of their interest in controlling their partners. The first subtype, dependent intimate terrorists, rank high on measures of emotional dependency and jealousy. These are men who are obsessed with their partners, desperate to hold them, and therefore jealous and controlling. They are not particularly violent outside the family. It is their emotional obsession with their partners that drives their need to control. The second type, antisocial intimate terrorists, show quite a different pattern, not being particularly dependent or jealous, but ranking high on antisocial personality measures and generally violent outside as well as inside the family. These are men who control their partners not because they are emotionally obsessed, but simply because they will have their own way, by any means necessary, at home and elsewhere.[28]

A rather different line of research has also confirmed Holtzworth-Munroe's distinction between two major types of intimate terrorists. The psychologists Neil Jacobson and John Gottman didn't just have batterers and their partners fill out questionnaires; they brought them into the laboratory to argue with each other. Although Jacobson and Gottman present a book full of evidence regarding the two types of intimate terrorists that they identified,[29] their most memorable findings come from machines that monitored the intimate terrorists' physiological reactions to arguments with their partners.[30] The men Jacobson and Gottman call "pit bulls" are men whose physiological reactions indicate powerful emotional turmoil as they verbally lash out in anger at their wives.[31] The men these researchers label "cobras," in contrast, are perfectly calm on the inside as they appear to lose control on the outside. When Jacobson and Gottman turn from the physiological measures that define these two types to other aspects of their behavior and psychological backgrounds, it is clear that the two groups correspond to Holtzworth-Munroe's dependent and antisocial intimate terrorists. The pit bulls are emotionally dependent and are desperate to maintain control over their wives, but are not generally violent toward others. The cobras are violent in other contexts as well as at home and are evidently calmly, calculatingly putting on a show of extreme emotion as they attack their partners in order to get their way.

What psychological picture of intimate terrorists emerges from all of this research on batterers? Although it is clear that there are at least two major types of intimate terrorists, the two types share impulsive personalities, an acceptance of violence, and traditional or even hostile attitudes toward women. The first two characteristics make them prone to violence, the third focuses some of that violence on women. But why their own partners? Here the two types differ. The dependent batterers are emotionally needy, jealous, desperate to hold on to their partners, and therefore controlling and violent. The antisocial batterers, in contrast, are controlling and violent because they must have their own way in encounters with anyone, including their partners, and they will coldly do whatever they need to in order to get what they want.

RISK MARKERS FOR INTIMATE TERRORISM

The use of the term "risk markers" in the domestic violence literature comes from an analogy to risk factors for a disease. In this case, the "disease" is being a perpetrator of intimate terrorism. There is a sort of a standard list of risk factors for domestic violence that is, unfortunately, based largely on general survey data, which we now know is mostly about situational couple violence.[32] The standard list is therefore useful only as a starting point for looking into factors that might be useful as predictors of whether a man will become an intimate terrorist.

Let me start with what has been described as "the most widely accepted risk marker for the occurrence of partner violence"—a history of violence in the family of origin.[33] "Widely accepted" notwithstanding, two recent reviews of the research on the relationship between growing up in a violent family and becoming a perpetrator of partner violence in adulthood indicate that the magnitude of the effect is so small as to be meaningless.[34] As Johnson and Ferraro point out, the commonly used metaphor of intergenerational "transmission" of violence is quite inappropriate. Even in what they describe as the "strongest intergenerational effect ever reported," 80 percent of the men whose parents had been severely violent do not grow up to be wife beaters.[35] The vast majority of men who experience childhood family violence do not grow up to be violent in their own families.

However, there are indications that research on the effects of childhood family violence is especially handicapped by the lumping together of all types of partner violence, and that experiences of childhood family violence might be more strongly related to intimate terrorism than to situational couple violence. Looking at the Pittsburgh data, for example, I find that there is a strong relationship between childhood family violence and intimate terrorism. The odds of a man being an intimate terrorist (as opposed to being nonviolent) were twenty-one times greater if his father had attacked his mother than if he hadn't.[36] A close look at Stith et al.'s review of this literature supports this conclusion; it appears that the weak findings the literature generally reports might not apply to intimate terrorism.[37] They broke down the studies they reviewed into those that used what I have called "agency samples" (dominated by intimate terrorism) and "general survey samples" (dominated by situational couple violence). The agency samples found effects of childhood parental violence that were three times larger than the effects found in general survey samples.[38] This combination of clear findings from my analysis of the Pittsburgh data (which did make distinctions), and hints from Stith et al.'s overview of the general literature (which did not make distinctions), suggests that childhood experiences of family violence may indeed be related to men's adult perpetration of intimate terrorism.

Now let's look at a risk marker for which the accepted findings are actually turned on their heads once we distinguish intimate terrorism from other types of partner violence: marital status. Family violence researchers have been puzzled for decades by the outcome of research designed to demonstrate that the "marriage license is a hitting license," as a feminist analysis would predict.[39] Instead, what they have fairly consistently found is that married couples experience *less* partner violence than do unmarried couples living together. Of course, once again, most of the research is done with general samples that are probably dominated by situational couple violence. However, Macmillan and Gartner's recent study that does distinguish between situational couple violence and intimate terrorism finds that being married increases the odds of intimate terrorism; in fact, the odds of being an intimate terrorist (rather than nonviolent) are 1.79 times higher for married men than they are for cohabiting men, even after controlling for a whole series of other variables.[40] In contrast, the odds of situational couple violence are decreased by marriage.[41] Thus, the puzzling results in this area are not so puzzling after all. On one hand, being married does reduce the situational use of violence by men who are not into controlling their partner. On the other hand, for some men marriage is a "license to control," legitimating their feelings that as husbands they are entitled to control "their women."

What about education, income, race, and ethnicity as risk markers for partner violence? As advocates for battered women often note, intimate terrorism cuts across all major axes of social differentiation. Men attack their partners in all racial and ethnic groups, and all social classes. Nevertheless, it has often been suggested that there are *some* differences in the likelihood of such attacks across various groups—and education and income are two allegedly well-established risk markers for domestic violence. Let's see if these differences hold up when we look only at intimate terrorism. With respect to income and education, agency data are probably not a very good source of information, because middle- and upper-class couples experiencing intimate terrorism are more likely than working-class couples to have the resources that make it possible for them to avoid dealing with public agencies. Nor are the Pittsburgh data useful in this regard, because the matching process used in that study pretty much guaranteed that there would be no relationship between social class and experiences of partner violence.[42] The data we need are available, however, in the National Violence Against Women Survey (NVAWS).

Beginning with education, there is a strong negative relationship between a man's education and the odds of his being an intimate terrorist, with the odds being decreased by 31 percent for each unit of education on the seven-point scale used in the NVAWS; this effect holds up strongly even after controlling for income and race.[43] Results are quite different for income, which has been touted as "an important risk marker for partner violence."[44] In the NVAWS data, income is not related to the odds of being an intimate terrorist.[45] We will see in chapter 4 that it is related to situational couple violence, which accounts for the general finding of an income relationship to partner violence in studies that do not make distinctions among types.

Race as a risk marker has had a checkered history in the domestic violence literature. Some scholars have found evidence that men's violence toward their partners is more common among African-American men than among whites, others have not; in many cases when differences were found initially, they were wiped out by controls for income or education, suggesting that the effect had more to do with socioeconomic status that race per se.[46] Of course, that earlier literature did not distinguish between intimate terrorism and other types of partner violence. I can, however, look at this issue using the NVAWS data; and the data are clear.[47] Looking only at blacks and whites, there is absolutely no relationship between being black and being an intimate terrorist; in fact, the odds for African Americans are slightly smaller than those for whites.[48] Once again, we will see in chapter 4 that the findings for situational couple violence are much more in line with the older domestic violence literature.

The previous literature on Latinos is similarly mixed, and it is now commonly accepted that differences among various groups within this category (e.g., immigrant versus U.S.-born or Mexican American versus Puerto Rican versus Colombian American, etc.) make the use of the kind of crude distinction available in the NVAWS questionable. Nevertheless, the NVAWS data indicate that although there are significantly increased odds for Latinos of being an intimate terrorist (about 2.4 times higher than for non-Latinos), the effect goes away when one controls for income and education.[49] This suggests that the effect is due more to socioeconomic status, especially education, than to any general cultural differences between Latinos and non-Latinos in the United States.

What about number of children, which is generally related to socioeconomic status and has been assumed to be a risk marker for domestic violence?[50] I find different patterns in the Pittsburgh and NVAWS data, a difference that I think is attributable to the social class controls that are inherent in the Pittsburgh data and the dramatic difference in sample size between the two studies (274 in the Pittsburgh study versus 5,000 in the NVAWS survey). The NVAWS data show a clear relationship between number of children and the odds of being an intimate terrorist, with each added child increasing the odds by a factor of 1.27. Although the effect is reduced slightly (to 1.24) by controls for education and income, this is still clearly significant with this large a sample. In Pittsburgh, where controls for education and income are built into the geographical matching design, the effect is actually quite similar (1.13), although not statistically significant with such a small sample.[51] There are two reasonable hypotheses about the origins of the relationship between the number of children a man and his partner have and the odds of his being an intimate terrorist. One possibility is that the stress of dealing with a larger family leads to violence, but I am inclined to dismiss this interpretation because data to be presented in chapter 4 indicate that there is no effect of number of children on situational couple violence.[52] If the effect were due to stress, one would expect to see it for both types of violence. The second interpretation assumes a correlation of number of children with sex role attitudes. It is likely that, after controlling for education and income, number of children is an indirect indicator of family traditionalism, which would in turn be related to men's beliefs that they should be the head of their household.

The Effects of Intimate Terrorism

The evidence is clear that in the case of male-perpetrated intimate terrorism the effects on the victim are dramatic. In addition to the physical injuries that are likely to be inflicted by male-on-female violence, there are longer-term effects on physical health, psychological health, and the relationship with the perpetrator himself.

Before I go into a description of some of the long-term effects of intimate terrorism, there is an important caveat—one rarely seen in the literature on the effects of intimate terrorism on the women who are its primary targets. Intimate terrorism, unlike most other violence, happens over an extended period of time and develops within the context of an ongoing relationship. Most of the research on effects is cross-sectional in design; that is, it involves a one-time comparison of women experiencing intimate terrorism with those who are not. It ignores the findings of in-depth studies of women's reactions to such violence over time, reactions that change dramatically from the first incident of violence, to the perception of a pattern, to attempts to change the pattern, to despair that things will never change, to preparation for leaving, and, finally, in most cases, to the escape. For example, our research using the Pittsburgh data finds that the level of injury caused by the first incident of violence is roughly the same for intimate terrorism and situational couple violence, while the difference for the most serious incident is dramatic. Thus, differences in the physical and psychological impact of the two types of violence may not appear until there are clear differences in the frequency and severity of the violence, and in the pattern of coercive control. As it becomes clear to the victim that the violence is not random—that it is enacted in the service of control—and as she is also subjected to all of the other control tactics involved in intimate terrorism, she may begin to experience the physical health impact of long-term violence, and the anxiety, loss of self-esteem, depression, and post-traumatic stress symptoms that have been shown to characterize intimate terrorism.

As we go through a description of the nature of these effects in the following pages, we need also to keep in mind that the vast majority of women who experience intimate terrorism do escape from it, either by changing their partner's behavior or by leaving the relationship. Studies of this process indicate that these women go through a series of changes in their perceptions both of their relationship with their abuser and of themselves that allow them to begin to gather the resources they will need to escape their entrapment.[53] And of course, once they escape or change their partner's behavior, they begin to heal physically and psychologically, as they move from being victims to being survivors.

But none of this happens overnight. Intimate terrorism takes place in relationships that already involve heavy commitments, and intimate terrorists further entrap their partners, using the very same tactics that they use to control them within the relationship. They are fully aware that they cannot control a woman who no longer "belongs" to them. Their threats to do violence to the woman, her (or their) children, or themselves if she tries to leave must be taken seriously when they are articulated in the context of the escalating violence of intimate terrorism. In addition, the psychological abuse is often designed to convince her that she has no viable alternatives outside of the relationship—that she is incapable of caring for herself or her children on her own. The enforced social isolation helps to reinforce his view of the situation, keeping her away from friends and relatives who might encourage her to start planning her escape, and the economic abuse cuts her off from the resources she may need to leave the relationship safely.

ECONOMIC EFFECTS

Interference with a woman's economic independence, including her ability to work and earn money, can impede her ability to exit a destructive relationship and achieve financial stability after escaping the relationship. In fact, economic dependency and lack of economic resources are among the most common barriers to leaving reported by battered women.[54] Keep in mind that in most cases women in such relationships must also assume that they will be economically responsible for their children after they escape from the relationship. Batterers create economic dependency by directly depriving their partners of access to economic resources, including family income and personal income, and by interfering with educational advancement that might make their partners more economically independent. For example, Riger and her colleagues found that 46 percent of the battered women in their study reported that their abusers had forbidden them to work and 25 percent reported that their abusers had forbidden them to go to school.[55]

The battering itself also hinders the job performance of women who do have jobs by affecting their health status and their ability to be on time for work and to complete required tasks. Research indicates that the abuser often purposely sabotages a partner's employment status by physically preventing her from going to work, physically injuring her so that she is either too debilitated or too embarrassed to attend work, promising childcare or transportation and then failing to provide it, destroying items/clothes she needs for work, harassing her at work, and causing her to be late and/or miss work, all of which may cause her to lose her job.[56] For example, in our study of women in a poor Chicago neighborhood, we found that for women experiencing intimate terrorism the odds of missing work because of health problems were three times higher than they were for either the nonviolent group or the group experiencing situational couple violence.[57] The economic dependence created by these effects is one of the factors that serves to entrap women in relationships with intimate terrorists, setting them up for the long-term physical and psychological effects discussed next.

PHYSICAL HEALTH

Four of our recent studies, using three different data sets, look at the injuries inflicted by different types of partner violence. They all find that for intimate terrorism the likelihood that a victim will be injured or even severely injured is quite high.[58] For example, looking at the Pittsburgh data, I find that 88 percent of the women experiencing intimate terrorism had been injured in the most violent incident, 67 percent severely. Johnson and Leone, using data from the NVAWS, found that 32 percent of the women experiencing intimate terrorism had been injured in the most recent incident of violence, 5 percent severely.[59] Remember, for the NVAWS these are the effects of just the most recent incident. In another study, Leone et al. reported that the intimate terrorism group in their sample (from a low-income Chicago neighborhood) was significantly more likely to have sought medical attention for injuries related to their partner's violence than was the situational couple violence group.[60]

The sexual abuse that often accompanies the physical violence of intimate terrorism (nearly half of physically abused women also report forced sex, and others report abusive sex)[61] also has health effects. In addition to the injuries produced by abusive and violent sex, there is increased risk of sexually transmitted diseases, including HIV. Abused women who have been sexually assaulted report higher incidence of gynecological problems. They have less control over contraception and therefore are at higher risk for unwanted pregnancies; the abuse, moreover, has been shown to be related to low birth weight and reduced weight gain in the first year of their babies' lives, both of which are significant indicators of a child's health.[62]

A history of such abuse and injuries also has general effects on health, as a result of both the direct effects of physical trauma and the stress associated with it. Extensive research literature now documents the impact of partner violence on a wide range of health matters.[63] Most of these studies, however, do not distinguish among types of partner violence and therefore probably underestimate the severity of the consequences of intimate terrorism because their group of battered or abused women includes other types of partner violence whose health effects are less severe. Studies that do make distinctions find that the health effects of intimate terrorism are (on average) more serious than those of other forms of partner violence. Leone et al., for example, found that the general health self-assessments of their intimate terrorism group (closer to "Fair" than to "Good") were worse than those of women experiencing situational couple violence, who rated their general health between "Very good" and "Excellent," a rating that was not significantly different from that of women experiencing no partner violence at all.[64]

Before I move on to the psychological effects of intimate terrorism, I would like to point out that physical and psychological effects might not be easily separable. A recent study by Cheryl Sutherland, with women recruited through newspaper advertisements to participate in a study of women's health, found that although injuries did have an impact on physical health, "[t]he stress associated with surviving an intimate partner's violence had a greater impact on women's physical health problems than did their injuries. . . ."[65] Cheryl Sutherland, Deborah Bybee, and Cris Sullivan, using a sample even more likely to be dominated by intimate terrorism (a shelter sample), found that the effects of level of abuse on physical health were almost entirely a function of psychological health effects rather than injuries.[66] Thus, while it may be convenient to consider the effects of partner violence on physical and psychological health separately, it would not be wise to think of those effects as unrelated to each other, especially in the context of intimate terrorism.

PSYCHOLOGICAL HEALTH

It is not unusual for victims of intimate terrorism to report that the psychological impact of their experience is worse than the physical effects: "I found the *verbal* abuse much worse than the physical abuse. . . . It was the constant verbal [attacks] that used to get me down more than anything."[67] They also often tell us that the psychological effects are more long-lasting than the physical effects, although there is evidence that once the abuse stops, the effects do fade over time.[68] The major psychological effects of intimate terrorism are loss of self-esteem, fear and anxiety, depression, and post-traumatic stress syndrome.

Self-Esteem. Considerable evidence establishes the effects of intimate terrorism on self-esteem, much of it derived from the qualitative data collected from women using the services of shelters.[69] Kirkwood devotes large parts of her research report to issues of self-esteem, reporting that "*all of the women* expressed the view that their self-esteem was eroded as a result of the continual physical and emotional abuse by their partners" (my emphasis).[70] Valerie Chang saw this loss of self-esteem as so central to the experience of psychological abuse that she used a quote from one of her respondents as the title of her book, *I Just Lost Myself.* Another of her respondents put it this way: "My self-esteem and self-worth and everything just plummeted. I just kept trying to be what he wanted me to be."[71]

Fear and Anxiety. One of Dobash and Dobash's respondents spoke of her chronic anxiety as follows: "I was frightened and I didn't want to cause arguments and I was trying to do things to please him so as it wouldn't start him off again."[72] In the Pittsburgh study, when the women were asked if they were afraid their partner would be violent again after the first incident, two-thirds of those experiencing intimate terrorism were at least somewhat frightened; 36 percent were very frightened.[73] Fully 78 percent "attempted to do what he wanted after that," and over 40 percent "tried very hard to please him."[74] Other quantitative studies confirm that fear and anxiety are frequent consequences of intimate partner violence; some studies with samples that are likely to be dominated by intimate terrorism,[75] others with general samples that probably include a lot of situational couple violence.[76] Even in this literature that does not distinguish among types, however, clues indicate that the fear and anxiety effects are largely due to intimate terrorism. For example, one study using the National Family Violence Survey finds that women whose physically violent partners had initiated the violence or subjected them to forced sex are the most afraid, and that women who had enlisted the help of shelters, lawyers, or therapists are more afraid than those who had not.[77] One can reasonably argue that all of these characteristics are markers of intimate terrorism.

Depression. Depression is considered by many to be the most prevalent psychological effect of intimate terrorism. Jacqueline Golding's 1999 analysis of the results from eighteen studies of battering and depression found that the average prevalence of depression among battered women was 48 percent.[78] However, because none of these studies distinguish between intimate terrorism and other types of partner violence, this number most certainly understates the effects of intimate terrorism. When Golding separated out studies done with shelter samples (likely to be dominated by intimate terrorism), the average prevalence of depression was 61 percent.[79] Our own study distinguishing intimate terrorism from situational couple violence using the NVAWS data found that 75 percent of victims of intimate terrorism scored above the median on a scale of symptoms of depression. The figures are 43 percent for women in nonviolent relationships and 65 percent for those experiencing situational couple violence.[80]

Post-Traumatic Stress Syndrome. Nightmares, flashbacks, avoidance of reminders of the event, hyperarousal. These are among the major symptoms of post-traumatic stress syndrome, a psychological disorder long associated with the traumatic experiences of war—more recently associated with rape and domestic violence. Daniel Saunders, studying survivors of domestic violence who were receiving services from shelters or other agencies (thus a sample probably dominated by intimate terrorism), found that 60 percent of survivors met criteria for a diagnosis of post-traumatic stress syndrome.[81] Our own analysis, using the NVAWS data, indicates that victims of intimate terrorism were twice as likely as victims of situational couple violence to score above the median on a scale of post-traumatic stress symptoms.[82]

General Prognosis. Lest we get too depressed about the impact of intimate terrorism on women's state-of-mind, let's remember that in most cases women do manage to handle even terroristic violence; they either escape from it or change their partner's behavior. In fact, in something of a silver-lining effect, it turns out that some of these negative psychological effects of intimate terrorism can be transformed by survivors into sources of strength and resistance. For example, Kirkwood's discussions with women who had left their abusive partners uncovered an important positive side of fear. Women's fear, and their anger about it, often provided them with the motivation and energy to begin to retake control of their lives.[83] The anger produces a transformation in women's understanding of their relationship with their partner (which we will discuss in the next section) and leads ultimately to resistance, both violent and nonviolent. We'll come back to this when we discuss women's resistance in the next chapter.

Some of my optimism also comes from the fact that survivors in the United States currently have available to them the services of over eighteen hundred shelters for battered women, in addition to all of the other apparatus of the general mental health industry. Data from follow-up studies of women who have escaped from such relationships indicate that most of them do seek formal help, and in many cases that help is quite effective. For example, recent work by Cheryl Sutherland and her colleagues found significant decreases in depression and anxiety eight and fourteen months after survivors left a domestic violence program.[84] And Cris Sullivan's innovative program providing trained advocates to work one-on-one with women to help them access the community resources they need has had dramatic results. Women who worked with advocates experienced less violence over time and reported higher quality of life and social support. More than twice as many women receiving advocacy services experienced no violence across the two years postintervention compared with women who did not receive such services.[85] Once women decide to seek help, effective help is often available. However, their decision to seek that help is largely a function of the changing nature of their relationship with their abuser.[86]

EFFECTS ON THE RELATIONSHIP WITH THE ABUSER

It is likely that any type of intimate partner violence will be related to relationship decline, and such effects have been demonstrated even in general surveys in which the relationship violence is almost certain to be primarily situational couple violence. For example, Testa and Leonard found effects of husband's physical aggression on wife's marital satisfaction in a sample of newlyweds—and the odds of separating during the first year were also affected by the husband's violence.[87] Research with agency populations indicates that intimate terrorism is ultimately destructive of relationships and that the vast majority of women eventually manage to escape their abusers. But just how different are the effects of situational couple violence and intimate terrorism on relationships? It is fortunate that the Pittsburgh study asked a number of relationship questions; I can therefore address this question using data in which it is possible to distinguish intimate terrorism from other types of partner violence. I'll begin with a few specific aspects of relationship quality, then move on to matters of general dissatisfaction and motivation to leave the relationship.

The violence and control that are involved in intimate terrorism take a dramatic toll on women's general enjoyment of time with their partners. In the Pittsburgh study, only one-third of the women experiencing intimate terrorism say that time spent together as a couple is usually or always enjoyable, as compared with 90 percent of women in nonviolent relationships and 80 percent of those experiencing situational couple violence.

Women experiencing intimate terrorism don't much enjoy sex with their partner, either. Nearly two-thirds say sex is unpleasant for them, compared with only 18 percent of women experiencing no violence and 28 percent of those experiencing situational couple violence.[88] Twenty-three percent of women whose partners are intimate terrorists say sex is often unpleasant. Over 40 percent of women experiencing intimate terrorism say they have sex with their partner more often than they would like, as compared to 20 percent of women experiencing either no violence or situational couple violence.[89]

As would be expected of women who articulate dissatisfaction with specific aspects of the relationship, women experiencing intimate terrorism also express general unhappiness. They are forty times more likely than women experiencing no violence, and eight times more likely than those experiencing situational couple violence, to report that they are not at all happy with their marriage.[90] Looking at the other side of the picture, only 3 percent say they are very happy—compared with 61 percent of the women experiencing no violence and 35 percent of those experiencing situational couple violence.

Ultimately, intimate terrorism will completely destroy the relationship. In the Pittsburgh sample, 96 percent of the women experiencing intimate terrorism said that they had at times wanted to leave their partner, compared to 23 percent of women in nonviolent relationships and 73 percent of those experiencing situational couple violence.[91] Nine out of ten of the women experiencing intimate terrorism had tried to leave their partner at least once (as compared with two out of ten in nonviolent relationships); 74 percent had tried more than once.[92]

The Ultimate Impact of Violence on the Relationship. Scholars who focus on the seemingly reasonable comparison of nonviolent with violent relationships are sometimes surprised to find what appears to be only a moderate effect of violence on relationship quality. Remember that most scholars are not making distinctions among types of intimate partner violence, and many are looking at data from general survey samples that probably include very few cases of intimate terrorism. Nevertheless, the data are interpreted as indicating the effect of "domestic violence" or "family violence" or "spousal violence," and everyone is surprised to find that perhaps half of these "women experiencing domestic violence" seem to be quite happy with their relationships. In the Pittsburgh data, 52 percent of women experiencing situational couple violence marked the top three categories on the ten-point marital happiness scale. However, when we make the distinction between situational couple violence and intimate terrorism, the picture is quite different. In the Pittsburgh data, only 10 percent of the women experiencing intimate terrorism marked those top three categories; 90 percent have tried to leave, most of them multiple times.

Qualitative studies of women who have sought help or who have left their abusive partners provide deeper insights into the process of redefinition that transforms poverty, injuries, poor physical health, low self-esteem, depression, and anxiety into actions taken to resist the control of an intimate terrorist and, if necessary, to escape from the relationship. Catherine Kirkwood provides what I think is the richest description of this process, for which she uses a metaphor of *spiraling outward from the web of entrapment*.[93] The process of spiraling outward begins with the woman's awareness of the major changes that we have just described above. Kirkwood reports that at some point the women she studied (women who had left their abusers) realized that they had changed dramatically from the people they had been—negatively so—and they began to ask themselves why that was. Ultimately, their answer was that their partner was the source of these major negative changes in themselves. This awareness produced strong reactions of fear and anger, emotions that provided both the motivation to leave the relationship and the energy to confront and overcome major obstacles to leaving. Unfortunately, leaving the relationship does not always end the abuse. For a discussion of the stalking and increased violence that can follow a woman after she leaves, see appendix B.

Incipient Intimate Terrorism/Nonviolent Coercive Control

A few years ago I found myself sharing a cab with a colleague on the way to a workshop on domestic violence and she told me a story (her story) that convinced me that in the study of domestic violence we can sometimes become too narrowly focused on the violence. She said she had been married to a man whom she would identify as an intimate terrorist, but that he had never actually been violent toward her until after she left him. He had exhibited all of the characteristics of intimate terrorism described above, except the violence. He controlled her every move, humiliated her at very opportunity, controlled the money and gave her a carefully monitored allowance, intimidated her with fierce outbursts of anger, and quite explicitly threatened her, including telling her in detail what he would do to her and her father if she ever tried to leave him. She said she knew what he was capable of and she lived her life in a state of constant terror. Wasn't he an intimate terrorist? When she did leave him he carried out his threats, attacking and nearly killing both her and her father. He is now serving a long prison term and she dreads the thought that he will some day be released.

Is this intimate terrorism? Well, the definition I use in this book starts with the actual violence, not the threats, and I suppose that is appropriate. This is, after all, a framework for identifying types of intimate partner *violence*. But her story made me think. It seemed so arbitrary that we would not call her husband an intimate terrorist before he actually carried out any of his threats, but we would call him an intimate terrorist if he ever even slapped her.

In our educational programs for middle school and high school students we describe intimate terrorism and then encourage these young people to be on the watch for signs of overly controlling behavior and to get out of any relationship that looks like it might be headed for intimate terrorism. Perhaps we need to take a bit of our own advice and add a concept such as "incipient intimate terrorism" to our lexicon of intimate partner violence.

An important recent book by Evan Stark makes much the same point more generally.[94] The major point of his complex, eloquently argued, and elaborately documented book is essentially as follows, although greatly simplified here: our heretofore narrow-minded focus on violence has often led us to miss the most important point—that battering involves a pattern of coercive control that is often much more debilitating than the violence itself. He argues persuasively that woman battering ("intimate terrorism" in my terms, "coercive control" in his) needs to be understood as a "liberty crime" rather than a crime of physical assault; a crime in which the victim is deprived of basic freedoms in her personal life.[95] Nevertheless, Stark's concept of coercive control, like my concept of intimate terrorism, includes violence in its definition:

> [A] course of calculated, malevolent conduct deployed almost exclusively by men to dominate individual women by interweaving repeated physical abuse with three equally important tactics: intimidation, isolation, and control. Assault is an essential part of this strategy and is often injurious and sometimes fatal. But the primary harm abusive men inflict is political, not physical, and reflects the deprivation of rights and resources that are critical to personhood and citizenship.[96]

However, his argument and mine both imply that even coercive control without the violence can deprive its target of her freedom and produce many of the same effects. The fact that such a pattern (coercive control without violence) is probably a major risk marker for intimate terrorism, requiring only the decision to add violence to the mix of coercive tactics, suggests the need for a concept such as incipient intimate terrorism.[97]

Fighting
Back
Violent
Resistance

Because intimate terrorism is perpetrated primarily by men against their female partners, what we know about violent resistance is mostly about women. Research from shelters and other agencies indicates that most victims of intimate terrorism do at some point react violently to their partner's abuse, and the heart of this chapter will deal with that violent resistance. However, before we focus on violent reactions to intimate terrorism, I think it would be useful to begin by briefly reviewing the evidence that female victims of intimate terrorism are working to cope nonviolently with the violence to which they are subjected.

Women Coping with Intimate Terrorism

Women resist their intimate terrorist partners. Women leave their intimate terrorist partners. Whatever the general public may think, researchers and practitioners who deal with domestic violence have moved far beyond the days when many professionals seemed to think that women didn't leave or resist. A few even believed that victims of intimate terrorism didn't leave or resist because they were basically masochistic, that they somehow needed the abuse.[1] Most, however, saw the alleged passivity of the victim as a consequence of the abuse. Lenore Walker, arguably the most visible psychologist working on behalf of battered women, theorized in her 1979 book, *The Battered Woman*, that victims of intimate terrorism had been abused into such a condition of submission that they were no longer able to act in their own interests; they were victims of "learned helplessness."

Less well known among the general public is the fact that just five years later Walker's next book, designed to verify her explanation of battered women's alleged passivity, clearly showed that battered women did not have low self-esteem or serious depression, did not have scores on psychological tests that indicated a feeling of helplessness, and were in fact quite active in seeking help.[2] Although Walker's second book certainly raised many questions about battered women's alleged passivity, the final nail in the coffin of learned help-lessness as characteristic of battered women was driven by Gondolf and Fisher's study of 6,612 women who entered fifty Texas shelters from 1984 to 1985. Their finding that "the majority of women made extremely assertive efforts to stop the abuse" led them to develop the "survivor theory" that now dominates our understanding of the reactions of women to intimate terror-ism.[3] The core idea is that battered women respond to severe abuse with in-novative coping strategies and active help-seeking.

In the twenty years since the Texas research was published, study after study has documented the strength and resourcefulness of women who are forced to cope with intimate terrorism. Each woman deals with such abuse in her own way, developing strategies for coping as she begins to understand what is happening to her and trying various means of changing her partner's behavior or protecting herself from his violence. Remember that this is vio-lence in the context of what began as, and may still be, a loving and committed relationship. It is not surprising, therefore, that most women do not simply pack up and leave after the first violent incident. They turn first to any of a va-riety of strategies for eliminating the violence, including simply confronting the partner and reasoning with him or otherwise challenging him, trying to accommodate him by changing their own behavior to avoid situations that seem to set him off, enlisting friends and relatives to persuade him to change his ways, seeking help from clergy or other professionals, or involving the police and/or the courts.

Because intimate terrorism develops within an ongoing relationship, often over a considerable period of time, women's coping strategies must be un-derstood within that changing relationship context. A number of researchers have identified general stages in women's reactions to intimate violence. For example, in research based on ride-alongs with police and interviews with women who have come to shelters for help or are in prison for killing their abusers, Kathleen Ferraro identifies four stages: ardor, accommodation, am-bivalence, and terror.[4] In another example, Jessica Burke and her colleagues identify five stages from their interviews with women who were in abusive re-lationships or who had recently left them: nonrecognition, acknowledgment, consideration of options, selection of actions, and use of safety strategies to remain free from abuse.[5] What the various lists of stages have in common is the recognition that women experiencing intimate terrorism go through a pro-cess of interpreting their partners' violence and then coping as they see fit, given what they think is going on. It is rare that a woman would immediately understand that she is dealing with an intimate terrorist. Most women first see the violence as a one-time, or at least temporary, anomaly (in most cases of situational couple violence, it would be), but in cases of intimate terrorism they slowly come to realize that they are dealing with a stable pattern of power and control. Remember that some of the tactics used by intimate terrorists are in fact designed to encourage interpretations of the violence that deny it or minimize it or blame it on the victim herself. Furthermore, the oft-noted cycle in which the violence is followed by a "honeymoon stage"—wherein abusers apologize for their violence, swear it will never happen again, buy flowers, and pledge eternal love—encourages women to see the incident as anomalous.[6] Ferraro's labeling of early reactions to the violence as embedded in "ardor" is a reminder that we are not dealing with stranger violence here, but with violence from someone you love. At this stage women may indeed "wish the abuse away" by minimizing it and denying the injury or defining it as situational or temporary. Ferraro puts it well:

> Physical violence is so inconsistent with expectations of an intimate partner that most women perceive the first instance as an exceptional aberration. A tremendous emotional commitment is threatened by recognition of battering, and most women protect that commitment through techniques of rationalization. These techniques draw on cultural scripts, excuses by abusers, and reactions of acquaintances and institutional actors to provide these women with accounts of the battering that preserve the image of intimacy between the partners.[7]

Nevertheless, in spite of the continuation of love and commitment in many of these relationships, as the violence of intimate terrorism continues women come to see it as a problem that must be dealt with.

At this point many (although not all) women try to control the violence by changing their own behavior. They do their best to figure out what "sets him off." At first they may focus on very specific behaviors, such as having dinner on the table or having everything just right in the morning. As one woman reported, "'He used to wake up in the mornings grouchy, and I used to have everything done before he gets up. . . . I always wanted everything to be clean and ready for him. . . .'"[8] However, because the goal of intimate terrorism is complete control, such small concessions are unlikely to be effective, and many women find that they have to transform whole classes of behavior. For example, many women report that they have had to broadly curtail their contacts with people other than their partners. They change the way they deal with strangers ("And then you can't even look at somebody walkin' down the street or road, and he'll get mad at you, tell you 'Get your @#% eyeballs back in your eyes'"), or talk to people, even their friends and relatives ("I didn't go see my relatives or my family. . . . I just started ignoring my friends"), or speaking one's mind ("I got so I didn't express my opinion, I found out how he felt about it, and that's what I'd say"), or speaking up at all in social situations ("It just got to the point where I don't say anything, if you say anything, he just starts yellin' at you").[9] Eventually, for some women the changes in their behavior are so dramatic that they have in effect lost "themselves" altogether— they are no longer the people they were before the abuse.[10]

Most women experiencing intimate terrorism do not try to cope alone. They turn to others for help. For information on how often this happens, we need to get beyond the studies that rely on agency samples, which, by definition, include only women who have sought help. General surveys that make the distinction between intimate terrorism and situational couple violence find that women experiencing intimate terrorism are highly likely to turn to others for help. For example, Leone's study of a general sample of women served by health agencies in Chicago indicates that almost two-thirds of women experiencing intimate terrorism talked it over with family (43 percent) or friends or neighbors (23 percent).[11] Even more striking, 70 percent had sought help from agency sources such as police, medical personnel, or counselors.

It is clear that battered women are not the passive victims they were once portrayed to be. They resist intimate terrorism through whatever means seem likely to help in the particular circumstances that they face at various stages in their relationship with their abuser. And for many of them this resistance includes violence.

Violent Resistance

It became clear almost immediately in the research on intimate partner violence that many women resist intimate terrorism with violence of their own. For example, Pagelow's early study of women who had sought help in shelters in Florida and California found that 71 percent had responded to abuse with violence of their own.[12] What is this violence? Although we have long known it was there, it was primarily alluded to in somewhat misguided characterizations of women's intimate partner violence as always involving "self-defense," leading to debates about how often women or men initiated violence. It is only recently that researchers have begun to give women's violence enough attention to distinguish its varieties, differentiating among intimate terrorism, situational couple violence, and violent resistance, but also acknowledging different kinds of violent resistance.

I have used the term "violent resistance" rather than "self-defense" because self-defense is a legal term carrying very specific meanings that are subject to change as the law changes, and because there are varieties of violent resistance that may have little to do with these legal meanings of self-defense. However, much violent resistance does meet at least the commonsense definition of self-defense: violence that takes place as an immediate reaction to an assault, and that is intended primarily to protect oneself from injury. This was the largest category of violence identified by Susan Miller in her qualitative study of ninety-five women who had been court-mandated into a female offenders program after arrest for domestic violence.[13] Miller classified an incident as "defensive behavior" if the woman had been responding to an initial harm or a threat to her or her children. Such incidents comprised 65 percent of her cases. Miller quotes one of her respondents:

> "I got to the point where I fought back at times, blocking parts of my body so that he wouldn't hurt me so bad," or after an assault ". . . I hopped in my car, and he moves behind my car and in front of my car and tries to break into the windows with a stick. So I tried to put the car in drive and pinned him up against the garage wall . . ."[14]

Another woman reported the following:

> "He was still mad at the younger daughter, so he went to push her and she used profanity with him, which she never had done ever, and he got upset with her and he started punching her. And I went to break them up, stop him from hitting her, and he hit me and I hit him back, and then he punched me and I punched him."[15]

Keep in mind that Miller interviewed women who had been arrested for domestic violence; thus, the 65 percent figure for defensive violence may not represent what is going on in general with respect to women's violent responses to intimate terrorism.

My guess would be that much of women's violent resistance is self-defensive but short-lived and does not lead to encounters with law enforcement. For many violent resistors, the resort to self-protective violence may be almost automatic and surfaces nearly as soon as the intimate terrorist partner begins to use physical violence. But in heterosexual relationships, most women would find out quickly that responding with violence does not help and may even make matters worse. As Pagelow reported in her early study, many women found that fighting back was ineffective. As one of her respondents said, "I tried to once and he really flipped out and beat me worse than ever. He told me that if I ever tried that again he'd kill me. I never tried again. I believe he would."[16] Indeed, National Crime Victimization Survey data indicate that women who defend themselves against attacks from their intimate partners are twice as likely to sustain injury as those who do not.[17]

A second type of violent resistance is what Miller calls "frustration response behavior." Although this category comprised 30 percent of the violence in her sample, I would judge from the accounts that Miller presents that some of these cases were actually not violent resistance, but rather situational couple violence, as frustrating arguments led these women to resort to violence with a partner who was not an intimate terrorist.[18] Nevertheless, it is clear that some portion of this category involved women being terrorized by their partners. In response they sought retribution, using violence not to protect themselves, but to get even. For example,

> "I acted out of the depression and pain that was inflicted on me from years of his abuse. That day . . . we kept arguing and he kept verbally abusing me so I got kind of heavy with the foot on the gas so he wanted to get out. When he got out, I thought, 'I'm going to give this prick a feeling of what he gave me,' so I chased him in the van."[19]

This is violence that is expressive of the frustration generated by abuse borne over a long period of time and, as Miller points out, has little effect on the power dynamics of the relationship.

Leaving

Ultimately, most women come to the realization that there is nothing they can do to stop the violence of an intimate terrorist. Their attempts to comply with the demands of their partner are ineffective, talking and reasoning with him has changed nothing, and responding with violence has not helped and may even have made things worse. They begin to consider leaving the relationship.

It is clear that most women who are faced with intimate terrorism do escape from it. For example, Campbell's research finds that within two and a half years, two-thirds of women facing intimate terrorism are no longer in violent relationships.[20] The evidence also indicates, however, that escaping safely from such relationships can take time. Intimate terrorists entrap their partners using the same tactics that they have used to control them. If a woman has been so psychologically abused that she believes that her partner really can get the courts to give him custody of the children if she leaves him, how can she in good conscience abandon them to him? If a woman has no access to money or a job, how can she feed and clothe herself and her children when they escape? If he monitors her relentlessly and isolates her from others, how can she get away and where can she go? If her partner has threatened to kill her and the children if she tries to leave, how can she leave safely?[21]

What women in such situations typically do is gradually gather the resources they need to escape safely, sometimes doing this on their own, more often seeking help from others. They hide away small amounts of money until they have enough to survive on their own at least for a while. They start working or going to school to develop a viable source of income, and they make plans with friends or a shelter to hide them during the period immediately after their escape. They involve the police and courts for protection, and they join support groups to help them with their transition to independence and with the emotional trauma produced by the psychological abuse. The process is not a simple one. Catherine Kirkwood describes it as a "spiral" in which women leave multiple times, only to return, but each time garnering information and resources that will eventually allow them to leave for good.[22]

The process is complicated not only by the intimate terrorist's determination to keep his partner, but also by the gender structure of institutions that may make leaving more difficult than it would be in a more equitable society. To a sociologist such as myself, the tremendous gender imbalance in the perpetration of intimate terrorism suggests important social structural causes that go beyond simple differences between men and women. For over two decades now, feminist sociologists have argued that gender must be understood as an institution, not merely an individual characteristic. Thus, gender theory incorporates gender at all levels of social organization, from the individual level of sex differences in identities, attitudes, and physical size and strength, through the situational enforcement of gender in social interaction, to the gender structure of organizational and societal contexts.[23] Part of the gender imbalance in intimate terrorism has to do with differences between men and women in their willingness and ability to use violence to control their partner, and part has to do with the fact that although general social norms regarding intimate heterosexual partnerships are in the midst of considerable historical change, they are still heavily gendered and rooted in a model that validates men's power.[24]

But more to the point here, as we discuss women's attempts to leave abusive partners, is gender as an institution; that is, the gendering of the broader social context within which the relationship is embedded. The social context affects the resources that partners can draw upon to shape the relationship and to cope with or escape from the violence. For example, the gender gap in wages can create an economic dependency that enhances men's control over women and contributes to women's entrapment in abusive relationships. The societal assignment of caregiving responsibilities primarily to women further contributes to this economic dependency, placing women in a subordinate position within the family and creating a context in which institutions (such as the church) that could be a source of support for abused women, instead encourage them to stay in abusive relationships "for the sake of the children" or "for the sake of the marriage." Then there is the criminal justice system, heavily dominated by men; this system is permeated by a culture of masculinity that has not always been responsive to the problems of women experiencing intimate terrorism, which was often treated as if it were situational couple violence.[25] On a more positive note, there have been major changes in all of these systems as a result of the women's movement in general, and the battered women's movement in particular.[26] Nevertheless, some of the women who find themselves in relationships with intimate terrorists come to feel that there is no escape, and they turn to a third type of violent resistance: murdering their partner.

Desperate Acts

The United States Department of Justice reports that in 2004, 385 women murdered their intimate partners. Although some of these murders may have involved situational couple violence that escalated to a homicide, most of them are the desperate acts of women who felt trapped in a relationship with an intimate terrorist. Angela Browne, in an important study comparing women who killed their partners with a sample of other women who were in abusive relationships, found that there was little *about the women* that distinguished them from those who had not murdered their partners.[27] What distinguished the two groups was to be found in the behavior of the abuser. Women who killed their abusers were more likely to have experienced frequent attacks, severe injuries, sexual abuse, and death threats against themselves or others. They were caught in a web of abuse that seemed to be out of control.

The level of violence and cruelty in many of these relationships is so unimaginable that I feel that the only way to convey the horror is to quote one of the many accounts that I had to review in preparation for writing this chapter.

You may want to skip the incident described below, from Browne's chapter "The Outer Limits of Violence."

> During the last year of one relationship, the man came home from work already upset. He grabbed and twisted the woman's wire-rim glasses and began gouging her eyes with them. Blood was running down her face, but he decided they should watch TV. He put a comforter on the floor and demanded that she undress; he wanted sex. Instead of using his penis, he used a squash; he said he thought she would enjoy it. Afterward, he made her take a bath with him and forced intercourse in the tub, banging her head against the tile wall. Then he had her sit on the couch in the living room while he went to the kitchen for another beer (his fourth or fifth since he'd been home). He tried to get her to drink it with him, and when she refused, he forced the bottle into her mouth, breaking off a tooth. He pushed her down and "f——ed" her with the bottle, pushing it violently into her vagina and anus. Then he drank the beer.
>
> The abuser went back to the kitchen—she thought to get another beer—but turned out all the lights as he returned. He made her lie down on the blanket while he fantasized about mutilation, threatening [horrible mutilations I'd rather not detail here]. . . . He often fantasized about violence, and she hardly listened. She was thinking mostly about her eyes; they were both swollen shut and the pain in her right eye was intense. She wondered if she was blind. Then she felt the coldness of a blade across her chest. This was the first she had been aware that he had a knife, and she was afraid to breathe. Still talking about what he was going to do to her, he began pulling the blade back and forth cross her nipples and her face. Somehow, being unable to see made it all the more terrifying. Finally, he put the knife down and forced intercourse in many different positions, some of them quite painful. . . .
>
> This incident covered a span of about six hours, finally ending in the early morning. The woman had a chipped front tooth and permanent scarring on her face and chest, and lost most of the vision in her right eye. She resigned from her job and quit going out socially. The doctor she visited in secret asked no questions about how she sustained such strange injuries. Because of her husband's position in the community, as well as out of her own sense of shame, the incident was never reported.[28]

Seventy-six percent of Browne's homicide group reported having been raped; 40 percent, often. Sixty-two percent reported being forced or urged to engage in other sexual acts that they found abusive or unnatural, one-fifth saying this was a frequent occurrence.

For many of these women, the most severe incidents took place when they threatened or tried to leave their partner, For example, after one woman fled to the police station and called a friend for advice, the friend called her husband:

> Hal was furious. . . . He took her elbow and walked her out the door and nobody intervened.
>
> All the way home, Hal was saying, "You goddamn bitch! You think you're going to leave me? When I get home we'll show you about leaving!" He snatched her over close to him, holding her clothes so she couldn't jump out. . . . When they got to the house, Hal came around and jerked her door open. He yanked her out of the seat and onto the ground, then began kicking her in the ribs. Each blow knocked Karen farther across the driveway. She knew she was sliding on her face, but there wasn't time to change positions. Finally he stood over her, daring her to get up. [Then he severely injured her dog, thinking he had killed it.] . . .
>
> Several days later, a friend helped Karen get to the emergency room of a local hospital. Karen had been in so much pain she could hardly breathe, and walking was difficult. They found that several ribs were broken, and there seemed to be damage to her spleen. The doctor was sympathetic and tried to get her to report it, but she told him, "That's how I got hurt so badly in the first place . . . trying to report it. . . ." After this, Karen was afraid to seek any more help. Instead, she began to think about dying.[29]

This is another major factor that distinguished the homicide group from women who had not killed their abusive partner. Many of them had either attempted or seriously considered suicide. These are women who feel that they can no longer survive in this relationship and that leaving safely is also impossible.

How does it finally come about that these women kill their partners? Contrary to the dominant image presented by the media, in which a desperate woman plans the murder of a brutal husband in his sleep or at some other time when she can catch him unawares, most of these desperate acts take place while a violent or threatening incident is occurring.[30] Although a few of Browne's cases involve a plot to murder the abuser, or a wait following an assault for an opportunity to attack safely, the vast majority of the final incidents took place in the midst of yet another horrifying attack. A few involved women

Figure 3. Intimate Homicide Trends in the United States: 1976–2004

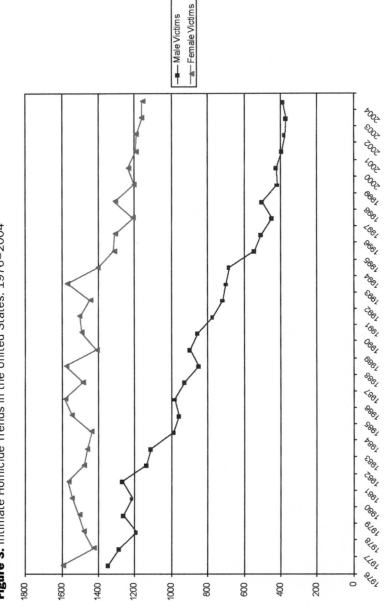

Source: James
Alan Fox and
Marianne W.
Zawitx, Homicide
Trends in the
United States
(Washington,
D.C.: Bureau of
Justice
Statistics,
United States
Department of
Justice, June 29,
2006). Available
at http://www
.ojp.usdoj.gov/
bjs/homicide/
homtrnd.htm
(accessed July 6,
2007).

using lethal violence in reaction to a direct threat to their child, many more took place in the midst of a particularly violent assault upon the woman herself, and others occurred when such an assault was imminent. Remember that these final incidents are the end of a history of escalating abuse and entrapment.

The Good News

Is it possible to end a chapter like this on a positive note? Look at figure 3. In the thirty years since the battered women's movement began to make alternatives available to women who were being abused by their partners, we have seen a dramatic decline in the number of women who feel that their only way out is to kill their abuser. From 1976 to 2004 there was a 71 percent decline in the number of men killed by their intimate partners.[31] It seems that the myriad support services that are now available to women experiencing intimate partner violence have made it much less likely that these women will feel that, ironically, their only salvation is violence of their own.

Conflicts That
Turn Violent
Situational Couple
Violence

Sometimes violence occurs even in relationships in which there are no sinister attempts to control one's partner or the need for one to resist such attempts. Intimate relationships inevitably involve some level of conflict, situations in which one partner wants what the other does not. In most cases such conflicts are addressed and resolved smoothly and routinely, so much so that many family psychologists now believe that such "normal" family conflicts have little impact on relationship satisfaction or stability.[1]

However, such conflicts are indeed the source of what is by far the most common type of intimate partner violence: situational couple violence. In any particular year, one out of every six married couples[2] and perhaps more couples who are dating or living together[3] experience at least one incident of this sort of violence in which a conflict between the partners leads to an argument, the argument escalates and becomes verbally aggressive, and the verbal abuse leads to violence. The violence may be relatively minor—a push or a slap—or it can be quite severe, even homicidal. This type of intimate partner violence, almost as likely to be initiated by the woman as it is by her partner, is the source of the misconception that women are as violent as men in intimate relationships.[4] While it is true that as many women as men acknowledge that they have committed at least one act of situational couple violence against their partner in the previous twelve months, this so-called gender symmetry is virtually meaningless in the face of dramatic differences in the nature and consequences of men's and women's situational couple violence. In fact, the data have always shown that among these violent respondents, men have engaged in more frequent violence during the previous twelve months and their female partners are far more likely to be physically injured, to fear for their safety, and to experience negative psychological consequences of the violence.[5]

What does situational couple violence look like? That is a much more difficult question to answer for situational couple violence than it is for intimate terrorism and violent resistance. All couples involved in the latter two types of violence share a central dynamic of power and control that produces the basic similarity discussed in the previous two chapters. In contrast to this relative homogeneity, the how and why of the escalation of particular disagreements into violence is much more variable. Situational couple violence is not driven by a general motive to control, but arises out of the dynamics of particular situations. In this chapter, therefore, I need to emphasize the fact that there are many different kinds of couple dynamics that can lead conflicts to turn to arguments that escalate to violence.

Variability in the Violence Itself

Unlike intimate terrorism, situational couple violence is not usually a central part of the couple's relationship. For example, in the Pittsburgh study we found that only 13 percent of the women experiencing situational couple violence were unhappy with their marriages.[6] In fact, over half of them were very happy. Eighty percent reported usually or always enjoying family time together, and this was not just about enjoying time with the children; 80 percent also reported usually or always enjoying time spent together as a couple.

People are often astonished by such survey research, which seems to show that many women are relatively satisfied with "violent" relationships, but it has to be kept in mind that for many couples situational violence involves only one minor incident, a conflict at some point in their relationship that escalates into an argument and then to the level that someone pushes or slaps the other, is immediately remorseful, apologizes, and never does it again. In fact, the intimate partner violence that is uncovered in general survey research generally involves quite a few "violent" couples who have been involved only in one or a few such incidents. For example, in a pioneering 1972 study of marital violence, Richard Gelles identifies fifteen violent couples in his neighborhood sample. Of those couples, 27 percent had experienced only one violent incident; another 40 percent had experienced only two to five incidents in the entire history of their marriage.[7] Although the Gelles study is small and does not involve a random sample, a similar picture emerges in large-scale research. For example, in the equally pioneering National Family Violence Surveys (the first large-scale surveys to ask questions about marital violence of a random sample of U.S. married couples), Straus and his colleagues report that 20 to 25 percent of "violent husbands" had been involved in only one violent incident in the previous twelve months.[8] That's as reported by wives; if we use the husbands' reports, the figure is 40 to 45 percent. The point is that for many couples who experience situational couple violence, the incident is an anomaly, either never or rarely repeated.

But situational couple violence is, in other cases, a chronic problem, with one or both partners frequently resorting to violence, minor or severe. For a look at the severe end of this spectrum, the Pittsburgh study is useful because it includes samples from the courts and from shelters, where we find the most serious cases of situational couple violence. One out of twenty of the men and one out of forty of the women perpetrating situational couple violence in that sample had been violent more than once a month during their marriages. As expected, such chronic violence is much less likely than it is for intimate terrorists, but it does indicate that situational couple violence sometimes does involve repeated incidents of violence.[9]

Data from the Pittsburgh study also show just how serious situational couple violence can be. Forty-three percent of the women who were experiencing situational couple violence indicated that their husband had become more violent over time. Although it may be reassuring that another 32 percent said the violence had decreased over time, the main point here is the variability, demonstrating that one cannot assume that situational couple violence is harmless: some of it is chronic and escalating. In the Pittsburgh study, 28 percent of the women who had experienced situational couple violence reported severe injuries.[10]

With this kind of variability in patterns of situational couple violence, from single minor incidents to chronic, severe violence, we have to ask the obvious question: Why is it that some couples have disagreements that regularly escalate into violence while others do not?

The Causes of Chronic Situational Couple Violence

We can start again with the standard list of risk factors for domestic violence that is based largely on general survey data. Because we now know that such survey data deal primarily with situational couple violence, this standard list is quite useful as a starting point for looking into factors that might be predictors of situational couple violence. I have decided, however, not to simply go through this list as I did in chapter 2, but rather to organize the risk factors into three general categories: sources of couple conflict, couple communication patterns that affect escalation to violence, and individual background and personality factors that affect escalation to violence. This organization is tied closely to the family violence perspective that was the basis of the first attempts to understand the causes of chronic situational couple violence,[11] and that was an important tool for interpreting the findings of general survey research on intimate partner violence.[12] Unlike intimate terrorism, which is deeply rooted in one partner's need to control the other, situational couple violence comes from the interpersonal dynamics of conflict management. The core assumption of family violence theory is that although all couples experience conflict, some are more likely than others to experience chronic conflict, and among those conflict-ridden couples some individuals and couples are more likely than others to turn to violence. The focus is on conflict rather than control.

The authors of that first National Family Violence Survey provide direct evidence of the relationship between conflict and violence. They asked respondents how often they disagreed with their spouse about five areas of family life: cooking, cleaning, or repairing the house; affection and sex relations; social activities and entertaining; managing the money; and things about the children. Only 9.4 percent of the couples reported no conflict at all in these areas. The relationship between amount of conflict and violence is quite striking for both husbands and wives, increasing from 2 percent of the husbands being violent in marriages with no conflict to 39 percent of those in the marriages with the most conflict, and from 2 percent to 33 percent, respectively, for the wives.[13]

SOURCES OF COUPLE CONFLICT

Relationship Status. You may remember from chapter 2 that there is more intimate terrorism among married than among cohabiting couples, the "marriage license as hitting license" phenomenon. The pattern is exactly the opposite for situational couple violence. In the general surveys in which the violence is primarily situational couple violence, researchers have fairly consistently found that cohabiting couples experience *more* intimate partner violence than do married couples. Macmillan and Gartner's recent survey goes a step further and distinguishes between situational couple violence and intimate terrorism;[14] they find that the odds of situational couple violence for cohabiting couples are almost double what they are for married couples.[15] I would argue that the most reasonable interpretation of this finding is that cohabiting couples are less thoroughly accommodated to each other than are married couples, yet have all of the same daily tasks of living together to provide potential arenas for conflict. It remains for future research to investigate the extent to which frequency of conflict mediates the relationship between marital status and situational couple violence.

Sometimes situational couple violence arises only in the context of a couple's breakup. Considerable attention has been given to this "separation-precipitated violence" in the divorce literature. For a brief discussion of it, see appendix B.

Money Matters. We found in chapter 2 that income is not related to intimate terrorism. This may seem to contradict the well-established finding that "[low] income, particularly poverty, is an important risk marker for partner violence,"[16] but as we have seen, the survey research that forms the basis of "well-established findings" regarding intimate partner violence really deals with situational couple violence. So, as I present some examples of findings regarding the effects of money matters on intimate partner violence, keep in mind that these data are not so much about the "working class brute" that often comes to mind in this arena as about the greater difficulty of everyday life for those who are poor.

The first National Family Violence Survey (conducted in 1975) found that the rate of "abusive" couple violence[17] for couples with family incomes under $6,000 ($23,280 in 2007 dollars) was five times the rate for those earning over $20,000 ($77,600 in 2007 dollars).[18] Now, here are some interesting things to pay attention to whenever you see such a statistic. First, the actual rate of couple violence for the first group was 15 percent. Eighty-five percent of these couples had not had a single incident of violence beyond a slap in the previous twelve months. Second, the rate for the more economically well-off group was 3 percent; that is, they were not immune to situational couple violence. Third, the effects of income on violence were identical for husbands and wives, reminding us that we are dealing with situational couple violence, not intimate terrorism.

The patterns for unemployment are similar. For example, in those 1975 data, 15 percent of the couples in which the husband was unemployed had experienced violence in the previous twelve months, compared to 6 percent of those who were employed full time. The stresses of economic marginality produce difficulties that can lead to arguments that can escalate into violence from either or both partners.

Children. What about children? Reviews of the literature do not indicate that number of children is a risk marker for situational couple violence.[19] However, the National Family Violence Survey found that among the five conflict arenas investigated, conflict over "things about the children" was the strongest predictor of partner violence: "Two-thirds of the couples who said they always disagree over the children had at least one violent incident during the year of [the] survey!"[20] So, the connection between children and violence is not number of children, but the handling of disagreements about childrearing.

Division of Labor. The findings for household labor are similar to those for children. There is no evidence that couples with a traditionally gendered division of labor are more or less likely to experience situational couple violence than are those with a less gendered division of labor,[21] but disagreements about the division of household labor can be a major source of conflict.[22] Even in 1975, quite early in the second wave of the women's movement, Straus and his colleagues found that "cooking, cleaning, or repairing the house" was the most frequent source of couple conflict.[23]

Alcohol and Other Drugs. Although the well-established connection between alcohol abuse and situational couple violence has to a large extent been interpreted in terms of the disinhibiting effects of alcohol,[24] there is considerable evidence that things are not that simple.[25] The complexities of the so-called disinhibiting effects of alcohol will be discussed below, but what I want to emphasize here is another possibility—that alcohol abuse is a source of conflict that can lead to violence even when both partners are quite sober. Using data from the large-scale 1985 National Family Violence Survey, Kantor and Straus show a strong relationship between the husband's drinking pattern and situational couple violence. For example, fewer that 7 percent of non-drinking men had been violent in the previous twelve months, compared with 19 percent of the binge drinkers. However, even among the heavy drinkers, alcohol was involved in the actual violence in only 48 percent of the cases.[26] Thus, for at least half of the incidents, the disinhibiting effects of alcohol could not have been a factor; and for the other half of the cases, disinhibition is only a possibility, not a certainty. Thus, it is highly likely that much of the effect of alcohol abuse on situational couple violence has to do with the arguments that are precipitated by one partner's objections to the other partner's excessive drinking.[27]

COUPLE COMMUNICATION PATTERNS
THAT AFFECT ESCALATION TO VIOLENCE

Although factors that increase the likelihood of conflict in a relationship do thereby increase the likelihood of situational couple violence, conflict does not inevitably lead to violence. All couples experience some conflict, but very few experience violence. For example, in the classic 1975 National Family Violence Survey, over 80 percent of couples with moderate levels of conflict had experienced no violence during the year preceding the survey. Even among couples with high levels of conflict, situational couple violence is more the exception than the rule. Over half (56 percent) of the couples with the most conflicts reported no violence in the previous year.[28] Conflicts may provide the "opportunity" for violence; communication patterns are probably the most important determinant of how those conflicts will be addressed.

The Role of Verbal Aggression. It has long been observed that physically violent relationships almost always also include verbal aggression.[29] But of course verbal aggression does not always lead to violence, and communication scholars have identified a number of factors that do increase the likelihood of such escalation.[30] Some of these factors are characteristics of the verbal aggression itself, such as the extent to which it involves an attack on central aspects of the self-concept or the extent to which the attack is public. Others are related to such personal characteristics as poor anger management skills or experience with violence. But perhaps the most commonly identified factor has to do with the couple's relationship. The so-called catalyst hypothesis posits that verbal aggression turns to violence only in the presence of general hostility and that in the absence of such hostility, verbal aggression may be "ignored or viewed as good-natured kidding."[31]

Verbal Skill Deficits. Knowing factors that lead verbal aggression to escalate into violence is helpful, but it tells us little about the source of the verbal aggression in the first place. In the previous section, we discussed some of the sources of conflict in relationships that might lead to arguments, but verbal aggression is more than mere argument. It involves a variety of forms of attack on one's partner, such as character attacks, competence attacks, or physical appearance attacks. What is it that leads an individual to turn to personal attacks rather than arguing the merits of his or her case? There is considerable evidence in the family counseling research literature and in the field of communications that one important factor is what researchers call "argumentative skill deficiency." The basic scenario involves a disagreement in which one or both of the partners lacks the verbal skills for dealing with conflict constructively. This skill deficiency leads the deficient partner to turn to verbal aggression as a means of winning the argument. A general norm of reciprocity in relationships then contributes to escalation, as each partner responds to verbal aggression with more verbal aggression. Such an escalation is most likely when both partners have skill deficiencies.[32]

Shared (Or at Least Contested) Power. Keep in mind that we are talking about situational couple violence here, not the intimate terrorism that is driven by control and that therefore probably has little to do with couple communication issues (see chapter 2). In one of the few communication studies that investigated different types of violent couples, Lenore Olson identifies one pattern of communication that involves an escalation to situational couple violence and that seems to embody the process of negative reciprocity, described above. She describes these relationships as having a "pattern of control . . . [in which] the shared control fluctuated back and forth between partners. . . . As a result, these relationships were fraught with power struggles, resulting in reciprocated aggression and violence."[33] She also points out that these couples described what communication researchers call the "wife demand/husband withdraw pattern," a pattern that is typical of the arguments of high-conflict heterosexual couples, in which wives try to confront their husband with the problems they see in their relationship and the husband withdraws to avoid the confrontation.[34] In these situations, wives sometimes report the use of aggression to get their withdrawing partner's attention.

INDIVIDUAL BACKGROUND AND PERSONALITY FACTORS THAT AFFECT ESCALATION TO VIOLENCE

Personality. Although sometimes the communication issues just discussed are rooted in the nature of the couple's relationship (such as general hostility toward each other), in other cases the problems may come more from the personal characteristics of one or both of the partners. Amy Holtzworth-Monroe and her colleagues, in a series of studies comparing different types of violent men with nonviolent men, found that the personality characteristics that distinguish intimate terrorists from other men (such as hostility toward women, impulsivity, antisociality, fear of abandonment, depression, and passive-aggressiveness) are not characteristic of men involved in situational couple violence.[35] In fact, on a whole range of psychological measures they do not differ at all from nonviolent men. Although in marital interaction they did exhibit less positive behavior, more defensive behavior, and higher levels of negative behavior, these communication patterns seem to be less a matter of personality problems than of skills deficits.[36]

Family History of Violence. Although a childhood history of family violence has been described as "the most widely accepted risk marker for the occurrence of partner violence,"[37] two recent reviews of the research on this "intergenerational transmission" of violence indicate that the magnitude of the effect is so small as to be almost meaningless.[38] The commonly used metaphor of "transmission" is hardly appropriate, given that even in the strongest such effect ever reported, 80 percent of the men whose parents had been severely violent had not grown up to be violent themselves. The vast majority of men who experience childhood family violence do not grow up to be violent in their own families.[39]

Education and Ethnicity. The relationship between level of education and intimate partner violence has had a checkered history, with some research finding that more educated couples are less likely to be violent, some finding the least violence among those of moderate education, and some finding no differences among various educational groups. As I pointed out in chapter 2, my own analysis of the NVAWS data found a fairly strong relationship of education level to intimate terrorism. A similar analysis indicates a much smaller (although statistically significant) relationship to situational couple violence.[40] Perhaps the checkered history of research in this area is due to the different mixes of various types of intimate partner violence in different studies.

Race as a risk marker has also had a checkered history in the domestic violence literature. Some scholars have found evidence that men's violence toward their partners is more common among African-American men than among white men. Others have not; and in many cases when differences were found initially, they were wiped out by controls for income or education, suggesting that the effect had more to do with socioeconomic status that race per se.[41] Of course, that earlier literature did not distinguish between intimate terrorism and other types of partner violence. You may remember that in chapter 2 we found no relationship in the NVAWS data between race and intimate terrorism. The relationship for situational couple violence is more in line with the older domestic violence literature showing African Americans more likely to experience situational couple violence than whites, but with the effect being due in part to economic status.[42] Although we can speculate about how much of this effect is due to the increased likelihood of conflict when one has to deal with racism in one's life and how much is due to a tendency for such arguments to escalate into violence, the current research literature does not allow us to differentiate between these two possibilities.

The Effects of Situational Couple Violence

The research literature on the effects of intimate partner violence on its victims/survivors has been carried out almost entirely with agency samples, essentially providing information only about the effects of intimate terrorism. A few recent studies of effects have made distinctions between intimate terrorism and situational couple violence and indicate, as one might expect, that the average effects of situational couple violence are much less severe than those of intimate terrorism. It is important, however, to remember that average effects do not apply well to individual cases. It follows from the extreme variability in the nature of situational couple violence, ranging from one minor incident to years of frequent physical assaults, that while the average effects may be rather benign, individual cases can be devastating.

PHYSICAL HEALTH

The few studies that have looked at the level of injuries involved in situational couple violence compared with intimate terrorism have found dramatic differences. For example, in the Pittsburgh study, only one-fourth of the women experiencing situational couple violence had suffered severe injuries, compared with three-fourths of those experiencing intimate terrorism.[43] Research using the general samples that are heavily biased in favor of situational couple violence also provide evidence of relatively low likelihood of severe injury, especially for men. For example, only 1 percent of the men in the 1985 National Family Violence Survey who reported being "severely assaulted" said that they needed medical attention. The figure for women is 7 percent.[44] This is not to say, of course, that situational couple violence is not dangerous. After all, one-fourth of the women in the Pittsburgh study had experienced severe injuries, and over half had experienced some level of injury. The risks are real, and especially so for women.

PSYCHOLOGICAL HEALTH

The findings are similar for psychological health. One study distinguishing among types of violence using the National Violence Against Women Survey found that although almost four out of five women experiencing intimate terrorism reported high levels of post-traumatic stress symptomology, this was the case for only 37 percent of those experiencing situational couple violence.[45] As with physical injury, the general survey research suggests that these psychological effects are more likely to afflict women than men. According to Stets and Straus, almost two-thirds of women experiencing severe situational couple violence report a high level of stress, compared with about one-third of men; 58 percent of women experiencing severe situational couple violence report a high level of depression, compared with only 30 percent of men.[46] Perhaps "only" is not best word here. The finding that over one-third of women experiencing situational couple violence report symptoms of post-traumatic stress and that almost one-third of men are depressed suggests that this form of violence *can* have long-term, serious psychological effects and that we need to investigate the conditions under which it does.

THE RELATIONSHIP WITH THE ABUSER

We sometimes see researchers expressing their astonishment that women whose partners are violent continue to stay with them and to report relatively happy marriages. As we saw in chapter 2, this is hardly the case for intimate terrorism. Such "surprising" findings are found almost exclusively in the general surveys that deal almost entirely with situational couple violence, in which the violence is, in most cases, far from a central feature of the relationship. Studies that do distinguish between situational couple violence and intimate terrorism indicate that, for most couples, situational couple violence does not need to interfere with the couple's relationship. For example, the Pittsburgh study found that only 13 percent of women experiencing situational couple violence reported low marital happiness and only 26 percent had repeatedly left their partner.[47] Again, we need research designed to investigate the conditions under which situational couple violence is a serious threat to the couple's relationship.

The Essential Variability of Situational Couple Violence

The most compelling pattern in the evidence regarding the causes and effects of situational couple violence is that of variability. This form of violence can range from one incident in the decades-long history of a relationship to chronic and sometimes severe violence that becomes a central feature of the couple's life together. Sometimes its root cause lies in chronic sources of stress and conflict in the couple's life that are no fault of their own; sometimes it lies in the psychological problems of one member of the couple, such as alcohol abuse problems or anger management problems. At times the problem has less to do with one individual and more to do with how the couple communicates. Some situational couple violence has almost no effects on the physical and psychological health of the couple or on the long-term status of their relationship, while in other cases it involves serious injury, long-term psychological impact, and the end of the relationship. Situational couple violence, more so than either intimate terrorism or violent resistance, involves a wide range of dramatically different phenomena that defy easy summary with averages. The next step in understanding situational couple violence must involve new research that looks into the differences among its various forms.

Implications for Intervention, Prevention, and Research

We have to make distinctions. It makes no sense to treat intimate partner violence as a unitary phenomenon. A slap from an intimate terrorist who has taken complete control of his partner's life is not the same as a slap from a generally noncontrolling partner in the heat of an argument, and of course neither of these is the same as the desperate use of violence by a woman who is being physically and emotionally terrorized by someone she loves.

The research cited throughout this book makes it clear that typologies of intimate partner violence are useful—even necessary—tools in domestic violence advocacy and research. In this final chapter, therefore, I will address some of the implications of differentiating among types of violence for intervention and prevention. But I need to start with a caveat. Although I will speak with some authority in order to avoid the distractions of constant qualifications and warnings about the need for further research, it should be kept in mind that research that makes explicit distinctions among types of intimate partner violence is still in its infancy. We still do not have definitive answers to many of the questions to which we need answers in order to make decisions about policy and practice with regard to intimate partner violence.

We can live with that sort of ambiguity in the world of social research. Science is, after all, a continuous process that is constantly involved in the correction of its errors and the refinement and verification of its theories. The use of those theories in "real life" is a much more risky proposition. In the area of intimate partner violence, people's lives are at stake, quite literally. So, as we consider the possibility of different interventions for different types of intimate partner violence, one theme must be central: safety first.

Implications for Intervention

Although there are many sources of potential intervention in intimate partner violence, including friends and family, I will focus on the formal intervention provided by agencies and professionals, including women's shelters, law enforcement, batterer programs, family court, and family counselors. I will also briefly discuss the importance of the coordinated community response teams that work to improve communication and coordination among all of the agencies that deal with intimate partner violence.

SHELTERS AND OTHER BATTERED WOMEN'S SERVICES

Thirty years of the battered women's movement has produced massive changes in the nature of interventions in intimate terrorism, with the major focus on providing protection and assistance to the victim/survivor.[1] There are now over eighteen hundred women's shelters in the United States providing a variety of services, including emergency shelter, support groups for both the women and their children, legal advocacy, individual counseling, and bridge housing, in addition to community education, social change advocacy, and the coordination of community responses to domestic violence.[2] Because of the visibility of these services, many of these agencies are known as "shelters," although most of them devote much more of their resources to other services. Staff at these agencies most often function within a feminist empowerment model in which they see their task as empowering their clients to carry out their own wishes.[3] They provide information and supportive services to help women protect themselves within the relationship, gain the financial independence that would allow them to leave if they so choose, file Protection from Abuse orders, join support groups with other victims of intimate partner violence, and generally gather the information and resources that they need to move toward a life without violence.

In part because the feminist theories of intimate partner violence that inform this movement have always focused on power and control issues, and in part because most of the cases that come to the attention of such agencies do involve intimate terrorism, shelter policies do not often involve distinctions among types of intimate partner violence. In general, interventions are based on the assumption that clients are dealing with intimate terrorism and therefore that the violence will be repeated and will escalate, and that the abuse involves many forms of control in addition to physical violence. The first order of business is the safety of the victim because intimate terrorism is the type of partner violence that is most likely to escalate to homicide.[4]

Nevertheless, it is important at least to acknowledge the different types of partner violence in initial discussions with clients. The common practice of defining "domestic violence" as intimate terrorism, describing it in terms of the Power and Control Wheel, may lead some clients (those experiencing situational couple violence) to conclude that they do not need help, that what is happening to them is not dangerous, is not domestic violence. The best practice, therefore, is to *explain the differences* among the types of violence while emphasizing that any type has the potential to escalate to lethal levels. Safety first.

My recommendation with regard to safety interventions in shelters is to treat safety issues no differently for situational couple violence than for intimate terrorism. Currently, the most visible shelter safety strategy is the provision of emergency shelter, often using twenty-four-hour hotlines through which women can make arrangements to bring themselves and their children to a secret or secure location for a period of time ranging from hours to months. When a woman enters the shelter (or contacts the agency by some other means), staff begin to gather the information they need to develop long-term intervention strategies. The first focus, however, is the development of a safety plan.

A safety plan is focused primarily on providing strategies and means for escaping if a situation appears to be heading for violence. The client is encouraged to gather and hide (preferably at some other location) the things she and her children will need if she must leave the house suddenly, such as money, clothes, identification, and so on. She also identifies a likely means of escape and a likely destination, such as the shelter, a friend or family member's house, the police, or a church—preferably a place where the abuser will not know to look for her. She may also identify a place in the house where she could securely lock herself and from which she would have the means to call the police.[5]

The staff will usually also discuss with her the possibility of filing a protection from abuse, or Restraining, order. Although these court orders are called different things and involve different nuances from state to state, every state in the union now provides a means by which women or men whose partners have been violent toward them can ask the courts to enforce a variety of restrictions on such behavior.[6] These can include making him move out of the house, stay at least a minimum distance from her and the children, forego all contact, provide support while the order is in force, or surrender his weapons to the authorities. Violation of the order invokes such penalties as fines and imprisonment, and provides the police clear grounds for arrest even in cases in which no crime has been committed. Can a restraining order stop a determined intimate terrorist from doing harm to his partner? Of course not, but it serves as a deterrent in many, if not most, cases, and it provides an avenue for swift incarceration in the event of its violation.[7]

This is where services for different types of violence might diverge, although only very cautiously. Some of the interventions indicated for situational couple violence might actually pose a danger to a victim of intimate terrorism. For example, couples counseling (often recommended as a remedy for communication skills deficits) would place a victim of intimate terrorism in the position of going into counseling sessions with a man who may kill her for telling the truth. My recommendation, therefore, is to assume intimate terrorism until it becomes clear that you are dealing with situational couple violence. It is usually the case that shelter staff work with individual clients over a relatively long period of time, during which they can develop a rich understanding of what is going on in their clients' homes.[8] Once the staff are relatively certain that they are dealing with situational couple violence, they could then begin to shift their intervention strategy by recommending individual counseling for one or both of the partners. The focus of that counseling would differ from case to case, with possibilities including drug and alcohol abuse programs, feminist education approaches, anger management training, or communication skills training. If, during the course of individual counseling, it remains clear that they are not dealing with intimate terrorism, and the relationship remains violence-free, then various couples counseling approaches could be considered.

Throughout this process, many of the services suggested for intimate terrorism would continue to be relevant for all clients. Support group meetings with other victims of intimate partner violence are extremely useful for those experiencing any type of relationship violence. Programs designed to promote financial independence that would allow a woman to leave her partner should she so choose are also relevant in all cases, and if a woman chooses not to leave her partner (which will be the case for many victims of situational couple violence), they put her in a better position to be treated as an equal within the relationship. In general, the services, support, and resources needed by victims of intimate terrorism are also of use to victims of situational couple violence. The major distinctions come in terms of such services as couples counseling that, while likely to be quite helpful in cases of situational couple violence, actually increase risk in cases of intimate terrorism.

LAW ENFORCEMENT

There have been massive changes in law enforcement approaches to intimate partner violence.[9] However, we continue to encounter cases in which such violence is treated more as a minor personal problem than as the crime that it is, and we must continue in our attempts to advocate for change in specific jurisdictions that have not yet gotten the message. Part of the problem histor- ically was that law enforcement often treated all intimate partner violence as a matter of situational couple violence, which wasn't seen as dangerous. This situation has changed dramatically in most jurisdictions, due to the educa- tion of the general public and law enforcement officials themselves—by the battered women's movement—about the dynamics of intimate terrorism, com- bined with successful lawsuits that cost police departments millions of dollars for the consequences of their inaction. All states now have protection orders and most police departments do regular training of their personnel with re- gard to the true nature of intimate partner violence. Similarly, prosecutors and judges are much more familiar with the dynamics of intimate terrorism and many jurisdictions now function with no-drop prosecution policies, in which batterers are prosecuted whether the victim wishes to prosecute or not.[10]

Although law enforcement interventions and shelter interventions have obvious differences (the former deals primarily with perpetrators, the latter with victims), they also have an important similarity: although most of the cases with which they deal involve intimate terrorism, they also deal at times with situational couple violence (in the case of the police, when the situational couple violence becomes violent enough or public enough that either the vic- tim or bystanders call). This overlap in types of cases encountered in shelters and in law enforcement is becoming even more striking. The now-widespread implementation of mandated- or pro-arrest policies in many jurisdictions has led to an increase in arrests of women for domestic violence, which means that law enforcement is now also dealing with more offenders who are essentially victims involved in violent resistance.[11]

It is hard to know the extent to which law enforcement is already taking into account distinctions among types of violence. The law itself is very much incident-focused, with arrest and prosecution presumably having little to do with the general role of violence in the relationship between the perpetrator and the victim. However, police officers do have considerable discretion in the decision to arrest, prosecutors in the decision to prosecute, and judges in sen- tencing decisions. It is clear from research on the decision to arrest that the police, often as a matter of policy, in effect make the distinction between inti- mate terrorism and violent resistance. The distinction is couched in terms of identifying the "primary perpetrator" in incidents of mutual violence. Although such a distinction might be focused exclusively on who initiated the specific incident under investigation, as police officers become more familiar with the relationship dynamics of intimate terrorism, information about the nature of the relationship between the partners may come into play. Judges and prosecutors presumably have more time than police at the scene to gather such information; as these distinctions work their way through the justice system, they will begin to play a more visible part in decisions regarding "alternative" sentencing, such as mandated batterer treatment.[12]

Restorative Justice. Before I move on to the discussion of batterer programs, let me say something about another alternative to prosecution and incarceration that has been used effectively in Australia, New Zealand, and Canada: restorative justice.[13] "Restorative justice" is a general term for a variety of intervention strategies that move away from the criminal justice system's heavily perpetrator-focused and punishment-oriented approach toward a more inclusive and healing perspective.

"Inclusive" refers to maximizing the active involvement of all stakeholders, including victims, families, and community members in addition to perpetrators. This inclusiveness is implemented in a variety of forms of "conferencing," in which the various stakeholders come together to discuss the nature of the crime and appropriate forms of redress. "Healing" refers to a focus on the welfare of all of these stakeholders, including the community and even the perpetrators. The strategies thus often include elements of apology and reparation, in many cases as alternatives to the penalties and punishments that would normally be imposed by the criminal justice system.

Concerns about the application of this model to intimate partner violence center on issues of victim safety and autonomy. They arise because of the general differences between intimate partner violence and most of the crimes for which the restorative justice model has been shown to be successful. For example, most of the crimes for which restorative justice approaches have been successful are "incident-focused," involving the injuries produced by a particular act such as a theft, destruction of property, or a single violent incident. Intimate partner violence, however, involves injury resulting from what is, or had been, an ongoing relationship between intimates, often a relationship in which apologies were part of the pattern of abuse. Another major difference is that most crime does not involve an established relationship of power and control between the perpetrator and victim, whereas power and control is often the central dynamic in intimate partner violence. There are other differences, but these examples may suffice to illustrate the concerns about the appropriateness of conferencing and mediation in cases of intimate partner violence. Is it possible for any of the parties involved to believe in the sincerity of an apology? Can we reasonably expect the victim to be honest in the face of a perpetrator who may have punished her severely for honesty in the past? Do we risk provoking further violence in response to what is said in the conference?[14]

Linda Mills has argued effectively for the implementation of a form of restorative justice intervention in some cases of intimate partner violence. In effect, she argues, as I have, that in cases of situational couple violence a restorative justice paradigm might be more effective than the standard criminal justice version of holding the perpetrator accountable through punishment.[15] She suggests the use of what she calls an "intimate abuse assessment team" to assess the case and make a recommendation about restorative justice (which she calls "intimate abuse circles") versus the more standard criminal justice approach. The assessment team is charged to evaluate whether "both parties are participating voluntarily and whether there is any risk of lethality if the more abusive partner is not incarcerated."[16] Although I would suggest a somewhat more conservative approach, in which the issue is safety rather than lethality, restorative justice approaches might provide a viable intervention in cases of situational couple violence.

BATTERER PROGRAMS

Batterer programs come in many forms these days, but the general experience with them is that they have minimal success. For example, one recent review of experimental and quasi-experimental studies of the effectiveness of batterer treatment programs estimates that, with treatment, 40 percent of batterers are successfully nonviolent; without treatment, 35 percent are nonviolent.[17] Although to some people that additional 5 percent nonviolent may seem trivial, the authors point out that this corresponds to forty-two thousand U.S. women per year no longer being battered.

The problem from my perspective is that studies of these programs' effectiveness do not in general make any distinctions among types of violence or types of batterers. It is possible that treatment programs are quite effective with some types of "batterers," such as men involved in situational couple violence rather than intimate terrorism. Another possibility is that different types of intervention work for different types of batterers. Although very little research has been done on this issue to date, there is already some evidence for differential effectiveness. For example, one recent study of almost two hundred men court-mandated to a batterer intervention program found that men involved in situational couple violence were the most likely (77 percent) to complete the program, with two groups of intimate terrorists falling far behind them at 38 percent and 9 percent completion.[18] Another study found that in a fifteen-month follow-up, only 21 percent of men involved in situational couple violence were reported by their partners to have committed further abuse, compared with 42 percent and 44 percent of the two groups of intimate terrorists.[19]

Another promising bit of research makes distinctions within the intimate terrorist group. In chapter 2 I noted that considerable research indicates that there are two major types of intimate terrorists: Antisocial intimate terrorists are sociopathic personalities who are willing to use violence to have their way in many situations, not just with their partner. Emotionally dependent intimate terrorists are not generally violent, but feel that they must take complete control over their partner in order not to lose her. In one of the few studies on the effects of tailoring the intervention to the type of violence, Daniel Saunders found that a feminist cognitive intervention was twice as effective for antisocials as for dependents, and a more psychodynamic intervention was twice as effective for dependents as for antisocials.[20]

I call this research "promising" because it suggests that tailoring our interventions with batterers to the type of violence in which they are engaged may greatly improve the effectiveness of batterer interventions. In fact, it almost seems that most current versions of batterer intervention programs are already tailored to the types of intimate partner violence identified in this book (see following paragraphs). Unfortunately, in general there is no differential assignment of different types of batterers to the different programs.

The feminist psychoeducational model that is the most common approach is quite clearly based on an understanding of intimate partner violence as intimate terrorism.[21] The approach involves group sessions in which facilitators conduct consciousness-raising exercises that explicate the Power and Control Wheel, explore the destructiveness of such authoritarian relationships, and challenge men's assumptions that they have the right to control their partners. Participants are then encouraged to approach their relationships in a more egalitarian frame of mind. As one author put it, this model "remains the unchallenged treatment of choice for most communities. In fact, the states of Iowa and Florida mandate that battering intervention programs adhere to the general tenets of [this] model to be state certified."[22] In most shelters and in many state and national organizations, "domestic violence" is *defined* in terms of the Power and Control Wheel description of intimate terrorism. Because most of the intimate partner violence that is encountered in shelters and in law enforcement is indeed intimate terrorism, this model is certainly the most appropriate if only one model is to be used. The problem is that, as noted above, these programs are not terribly effective across the board, and there may be more effective models for some of the batterers who come to programs through these avenues.

Some men report that they are insulted by these feminist programs that assume that they are determined to completely control their partners' lives.[23] If, in fact, they are involved in situational couple violence and not intimate terrorism, then the second major type of batterer program may be what they need. Cognitive behavioral groups focus on interpersonal skills that sound like a list developed from our discussion in chapter 4 of the processes by which a couple's arguments can escalate to verbal aggression and ultimately to violence. These batterer groups teach anger management techniques, some of which are interpersonal (such as timeouts), others of which are cognitive (such as avoiding negative attributions about their partners' behaviors). They also practice exercises designed to develop their members' communication skills and ability to assert themselves without becoming aggressive. Although these techniques are also used by marriage counselors, couple approaches are almost never recommended for batterer programs because of the threat they might pose to victims of intimate terrorism. Thus, in batterer programs these cognitive behavioral interventions are implemented primarily with groups of male batterers rather than with couples.

One relatively new development in batterer intervention is a consequence of dramatic increases in arrests of women for intimate partner violence in jurisdictions that have implemented mandated-arrest policies. Although on the surface many of these groups appear to function much like the groups for men, research into how they actually function suggests that at least some of them assume that many of their participants are involved in violent resistance.[24] They seem to function much like shelter support groups for victims of intimate terrorism, encouraging the development of safety plans and providing skills for coping with their partners' violence within the relationships.

Given that these different approaches appear to be targeted to the major types of intimate partner violence, it seems reasonable to develop some sort of triage system by which different types of "batterers" would be offered different types of interventions. It may also be useful to differentiate even more finely. For example, for some batterers involved in situational couple violence, the problem is communication skills; while for others, it may be alcohol abuse. Similarly, for some intimate terrorists the problems are deeply psychological and call for a fairly psychodynamic approach to treatment; while for others, the problem is more one of an antisocial or misogynistic attitude that would be more responsive to a feminist psychoeducational approach. In all cases, of course, holding batterers accountable for their violent behavior in the criminal justice system provides essential motivation for change.

FAMILY COURT AND CHILD PROTECTIVE SERVICES

I treat family court and child protective services together because, although intimate partner violence is often an issue even in divorces that do not involve children, the major policy concerns regarding such violence in family courts have focused on matters of child custody. Thus, many of the same issues raised in divorce courts are also raised in child protection agencies. The general policy question has often boiled down to "Should every parent who has been violent toward his or her partner lose custody of his or her children?" Lying behind this simple view of the issue are two questions: (1) What is the impact of intimate partner violence on children in cases in which neither parent is violent toward the children? and (2) What is the likelihood that someone who is violent toward his or her partner will also be violent toward the children? The answer to both questions is that it depends upon what type of violence you are talking about.[25]

Those who argue that there is a link between intimate partner violence and child abuse are generally (and tacitly) referring to intimate terrorism, not situational couple violence. Everyone seems to agree that there is a link between intimate terrorism and child abuse. What we do not know is the extent to which there is or is not a link between situational couple violence and child abuse. It seems likely to me that the sampling biases of various studies account for the wildly different estimates of the overlap between intimate partner violence and child abuse—from 6 percent to 100 percent, according to one discussion of that literature.[26] I expect that the 6 percent findings involve situational couple violence or violent resistance; the 100 percent findings, intimate terrorism. If, as I expect, research establishes that violent resistance and situational couple violence are not strongly linked to the risk of child abuse, then the courts and child protective services will have support for the recent movement to make such distinctions in deliberations about child custody in specific cases.[27]

It is important that we do child custody assessments carefully. We need to assess women's violence as well as men's, and, most importantly, we need to make distinctions among types of violence. In the case of a custody battle between an intimate terrorist and a partner who is resisting with violence, although both parents have been violent, the primary risk to the children is the intimate terrorist. In cases of situational couple violence, there may not be any increased risk to the children. If the situational couple violence is singular and mild, perhaps there is no problem; if the violence is chronic or severe, I would argue that what is needed is a more nuanced analysis of the situational causes of the violence. If one partner has an anger management problem, then he or she is the parent most at risk for child abuse. If the problem is one of couple communication or chronic conflict over one or a few issues, generalization to child abuse is unlikely. The issues are complicated and differ depending on the type of violence, but one thing is clear: the assessment of the violence must include information about its role in the relationship between the contesting parties. A narrow focus on acts of violence will not suffice.[28]

There is a further complication of the overly simplistic question I originally posed about violent parents' losing custody of their children. The courts and child protective services often have more nuanced choices available to them than custody/no custody. One very thorough discussion of the range of co-parenting options in the case of divorce child-custody disputes distinguishes among five different possible outcomes.[29] (1) Coparenting generally involves joint custody in which both parents are involved in making cooperative decisions about the child's welfare. (2) In parallel parenting, both parents are involved in the child's life, but the arrangement is designed to minimize contact between the parents, thus minimizing the potential for continued conflict. (3) Supervised exchange has to do with organizing the movement of the child from parent to parent in a manner that minimizes the potential for parental conflict related to the exchange. (4) Supervised access is recommended in cases in which one or both parents does seem to pose a temporary danger to the child; access is provided only under direct supervision in specialized centers and/or by trained personnel. The hope is that the conditions that led to supervised access will be resolved and the parent can proceed to a more normal parent-child relationship. (5) In the most serious cases, in which a parent poses an ongoing risk to the child, all contact with the child would be prohibited.

We need to err on the side of safety in these matters. As I suggested above with regard to shelter decisions, it is probably wise to assume that all violence is intimate terrorism until proven otherwise. Once the resources are invested that can establish some of the nuances of the individual case, then more nuanced responses can be considered.

COORDINATED COMMUNITY RESPONSE

The list of arenas, above, in which distinctions among types of intimate partner violence must be taken into account is certainly not complete. Many other professionals encounter intimate partner violence in the course of their work either in the schools, in religious institutions, in medical facilities, or in marriage and psychological counseling services, to name just a few. One very promising development that involves the recognition that intimate partner violence touches the lives of many people in every community is the concept of a coordinated community response to such violence. Many communities worldwide have formed task forces in which representatives of various sectors of the community coordinate their efforts to intervene effectively in intimate partner violence when it does occur and, perhaps even more importantly, engage in coordinated educational activities aimed at prevention.[30]

Implications for Prevention

Activities focused on the prevention of intimate partner violence involve a combination of deterrence through holding violent partners accountable in the criminal justice system, education about intimate partner violence, and targeting general social structures and cultural practices that support intimate partner violence.

The criminal justice system has experienced an almost complete turnaround in its approach to intimate partner violence in just thirty years. We have moved from a situation in which such violence was treated as a private, family matter to be kept out of the criminal justice system whenever possible to a situation in which most jurisdictions have mandatory-arrest policies that require criminal justice intervention whenever there is clear evidence of intimate partner violence. Such intervention serves as a deterrent not only for those who are adjudicated and those who might be tempted to use violence, but also serves to reinforce a general cultural atmosphere in which violence against one's intimate partner is considered a social problem that calls for outside intervention.

Educational efforts and social change advocacy to prevent intimate partner violence have long been major parts of the shelter system that grew out of the battered women's movement.[31] So-called shelters do much more than provide temporary emergency shelter and other forms of support for victims of intimate partner violence. In most cases, they are also engaged in widespread community education involving everything from programs in schools to social change advocacy in specific institutions (such as law enforcement or health care) to general media appearances. Most of this effort is focused on intimate terrorism. Education with regard to situational couple violence takes place more in the context of marriage preparation courses conducted either in conjunction with religious institutions or with government-sponsored healthy relationship initiatives.[32]

General social change advocacy has focused on two major cultural issues: gender inequality, and a culture of violence. The battered women's movement, concerned primarily with intimate terrorism, has always identified patriarchal social structures as one major source of intimate partner violence. This movement has, therefore, always seen its task as going beyond providing support for victims of such violence, to changing cultural ideas that support men's domination of women and changing the structure of gender inequality that contributes to the entrapment of women in relationships with abusive men. Family violence researchers have focused more on advocating for changes in the cultural legitimation of violence in general, arguing that support for violence pervades U.S. culture. Such support is seen in the media obsession with violence and in the widespread acceptance of practices such as spanking in the home.

Implications for Research

The distinctions among intimate terrorism, violent resistance, and situational couple violence are compelling. Once they are made, they seem like nothing less that simple common sense. Talk to women's advocates who work in shelters and they tell you, "Yes, we see these distinctions all the time. Although the violent women who come to us are mostly involved in violent resistance against intimate terrorist partners who are terrorizing them in their own homes and from whom they cannot escape, we do see some women whose partners do not seem to be overly controlling, who simply get drunk or lose their tempers and do horrible things. And these women need our help, too, as do the few who seem to be as much involved in creating the violence in their relationship as are their partners."

Interview violent men in prison and it is clear that most of them are intimate terrorists who felt that to be men or to keep the women they loved, they had to have complete control, even if it meant using violence to have their way. Talk to women in prison who have been violent toward their partners and you find that most of them were involved in violent resistance. But talk to marriage counselors and you hear about a lot of couples in which arguments simply get out of hand, leading to violence—sometimes lethal violence. Sure, they see the occasional intimate terrorist in their practices, but mostly they see couples who need help in finding nonviolent ways to work out their differences.

As we have seen throughout this book, the differences between the research findings in general samples dominated by situational couple violence and those in agency samples dominated by intimate terrorism are quite convincing. The few studies in which the right questions have been asked show clearly that these forms of violence are dramatically different phenomena— and those studies were done by a number of researchers, in different disciplines, using different ways of operationalizing the distinctions. When this sort of triangulation takes place in science, we can be fairly confident that what we have found is real—not the product of one researcher's biases.

But the truth is that these distinctions are quite recent in the history of research on intimate partner violence, as discussed in the introduction. I could cite very few studies that were specifically designed to answer even the most basic questions about the differences among intimate terrorism, violent resistance, and situational couple violence. Unfortunately, scholarly papers continue to be published that ignore these distinctions, lumping together all violent men or violent couples or violent women and making sweeping pronouncements about the nature of intimate partner violence. A few researchers cling to the idea that women are as violent as men in close relationships, basing their pronouncements about battered husbands on research that deals with situational couple violence, which so rarely involves the serious violence or the pattern of control that we identify with "battering." The talk shows and other media pick up on these pronouncements and bring in the rare stories of "girls who beat up their boyfriends," contributing to the confusion about the different realities of violence in intimate relationships.

We desperately need a concerted effort to redress the imbalance of thirty years of research by hundreds of scholars who did not make these distinctions vs. a few years of research by a few scholars who did. We need research designed to give us clear answers to the many questions that have been raised throughout this book. What is the difference in the impact on children of intimate terrorism and situational couple violence? Are same-sex couples as likely to be involved in intimate terrorism as heterosexual couples? In situational couple violence? What are the best treatments for the male intimate terrorists (and the few women) who want to stop their violence? How can we help individuals and couples whose arguments tend to escalate into violence? Do intimate terrorists who are arrested stop being violent? What are the outcomes for men or women who were arrested for situational couple violence or violent resistance? Should women involved in violent resistance suffer the same penalties or receive the same mandated batterer treatment as men who are intimate terrorists or men and women who are involved in situational couple violence? Are children who are exposed to their parents' situational couple violence at serious risk of long-term psychological harm? Is gender inequality an important factor in intimate terrorism? Situational couple violence? What kind of impact do cultures of violence or of nonviolence have on these different types of personal violence?

The distinctions laid out in this book provide the framework for answering these and many other such questions. For the most part the research has yet to be done. We need to demand that every piece of research on intimate partner violence be planned so that distinctions among types of violence are built into the research design; with a concerted effort we should be able fairly quickly to move our understanding of intimate partner violence to the next level, helping us to design effective social policies and to intervene usefully in the violence that continues to be a factor in so many close relationships around the world.

Appendix A

Identifying Intimate
Terrorism and Other Types
of Partner Violence

The task of identifying the different types of intimate partner
violence seems simple on the face of it. You start by finding out if the individual is violent, then you look into whether that violence is accompanied by a
general pattern of coercive control, and you place all of this information in the
context of the same information about his or her partner. If the individual is
violent and controlling, but his or her partner is not, then you are looking at
an intimate terrorist. If his or her partner is also violent and controlling, then
you are dealing with a rare case of mutual violent control. If the individual is
violent but not controlling, then you look at the partner's behaviors to determine whether you are dealing with violent resistance or situational couple violence. If the partner is an intimate terrorist, you have violent resistance. If the
partner is not, you have situational couple violence. Simple. The hard part is
deciding who is controlling and who is not.

Measuring Coercive Control

Control is a continuum. Everyone "controls" their partner to some extent
in an intimate relationship; after all, a relationship by definition involves mutual influence. What we need is a way to assess the amount of *coercive* control
that an individual exercises in the relationship. Mary Ann Dutton and Lisa
Goodman have recently provided an excellent analysis of the elements of coercive control, which is discussed in detail in chapter 1. Briefly, they argue that
coercion involves getting someone to do something they do not want to do by
"using or threatening . . . negative consequences for noncompliance."[1]

Dutton and Goodman's analysis of the essential process of coercive control
reveals that it involves most of the tactics commonly identified by battered
women as features of their batterers' behaviors. That effective coercive control
requires that the perpetrator make it clear that he/she is willing and able to
impose punishment if "necessary." This is where the threats and intimidation
reported by battered women come in. Threats such as "If you try to leave me,

I'll kill you and the children" make the contingency and willingness to punish clear: "If you stay, nothing will happen; if you don't, you'll pay for it." Or the children might be used in threats to take custody of them if the partner leaves. Intimidation, through the destruction of property or through attacks on pets, makes it clear that the intimate terrorist is not only willing but able to use violence. A damaged wall or destroyed piece of furniture demonstrates the physical ability to do serious damage. Coercive control also requires surveillance. In order to punish for "misbehavior," the intimate terrorist has to monitor his or her partner's behavior.

Another basic element of coercive control is wearing down the partner's resistance; intimate terrorists use a variety of tactics to undermine their partner's willingness or ability to fight for freedom from control. With respect to the will to resist, the actual violence and the threats and intimidation can induce a "terror" that keeps partners from resisting; but intimate terrorists also use more subtle techniques, many of which involve the forms of emotional and psychological abuse that have been the focus of so much research in psychology and social work.[2] A related tactic for reducing the will to resist is legitimation, convincing the partner that the intimate terrorist has the right to control and punish. Legitimation may take the form of an assertion of status as head of household. Or it might be closely tied up with the psychological attacks on self-esteem just discussed above, as in, "You are so incompetent and useless that I have to take control." This tactic may then lead to blaming the violence on her—if only she could do her job, or behave herself, or understand his needs, etc., then he wouldn't drink, lose control, have to punish her, or whatever his excuses are for the use of violence. With regard to the ability to resist, intimate terrorists do what they can to cut their partner off from the resources required for effective resistance, including money, education, and social support.

Dutton and Goodman have devised measures of the various elements of coercive control enumerated in their model.[3] Unfortunately, their current approach involves ninety-two items, probably too unwieldy for most purposes. However, as I noted in chapter 1, Dutton and Goodman's analysis essentially adds up to the list of control tactics enumerated by Pence and Paymar in the Power and Control Wheel;[4] Graham-Kevan and Archer have recently devised a twenty-four-item measure of coercive control based on the work of Pence and Paymar.[5] This measure yields separate scores for each of five subscales and a summary score of coercive control. The scale, called the Controlling Behaviors Scale, has now been used in a number of studies with a variety of different samples; and Graham-Kevan and Archer report alphas in the range of .82–.90.[6]

Threats are assessed by four items: (1) "Did you/your partner make or carry out threats to do something to harm the other;" (2) "Did you/your partner threaten to leave the other and/or commit suicide?" (3) "Did you/your partner threaten to report the other to welfare?" (4) "Did you/your partner encourage the other to do illegal things he/she would not otherwise have done?" *Intimidation* is assessed by five items: (1) "Did you/your partner use looks, actions, and/or gestures to change the other's behaviour?" (2) "If **yes**, did you/your partner make the other afraid when this was done?" (3) "Did you/your partner smash property when annoyed/angry?" (4) "If **yes**, was it the other's property?" (5) "When angry did you/your partner vent anger on household pets?" *Economic control* is assessed by five items: (1) "Did you/your partner disapprove of the other working or studying?" (2) "If **yes**, did you/your partner try and prevent or make difficult the other working or studying?" (3) "Did you/your partner feel it was necessary to have control of the other's money (e.g., wage, benefit)?" (4) "If **yes**, did you/your partner give the other an allowance/require other to ask for money?" (5) "Did you/your partner have knowledge of the family income? *Emotional control* is assessed by five items: (1) "Did you/your partner put the other down when they felt the other was getting 'too big for their boots'?" (2) "If **yes**, did you/your partner put the other down in front of others (friends, family, children);" (3) "Did you/your partner try to humiliate the other in front of others?" (4) "Did you/your partner tell the other that he/she was going crazy?" (5) "Did you/your partner call the other unpleasant names?" Finally, *isolation* is assessed by five items: (1) "Did you/your partner restrict the amount of time the other spent with friends and/or family?" (2) "If you/your partner went out did the other want to know where the other went and who the other spoke to?" (3) "Did you/your partner limit the other's activities outside the relationship?" (4) "Did you/your partner feel suspicious and jealous of the other?" (5) "If **yes**, was this used as a reason to monitor and control the other's activities?"

Another useful measure of coercive control is Tolman's somewhat misnamed Psychological Maltreatment of Women Inventory (PMWI), of which there is a fourteen-item short form.[7] The PMWI is composed of two subscales designed to measure dominance-isolation and emotional-verbal psychological abuse. It has been widely used in the study of intimate partner violence, although not always recognized as a measure of coercive control.

Finally, given that even fourteen items may seem excessive to many survey researchers, one might consider the set of items that has been used in both the Canadian and United States' violence against women surveys.[8] The seven items are each prefaced by "Thinking about your current [husband/wife/etc.], would you say [he/she] . . . ?" The following control tactics are addressed: (1) "tries to limit your contact with family and friends?" (2) "is jealous or possessive?" (3) "insists on knowing who you are with at all times?" (4) "calls you names or puts you down in front of others?" (5) "makes you feel inadequate?" (6) "shouts or swears at you?" (7) "prevents you from knowing about or having access to the family income even when you ask?"

Identifying High Coercive Control

Now comes the problem of deciding what comprises high coercive control. Each of the scales discussed above produces a continuum of coercive control that must be dichotomized if one is to create the proposed typology of intimate partner violence. One approach that I have used, as have Graham-Kevan and Archer, is cluster analysis. Cluster analysis essentially creates clusters of individuals who have similar profiles on a set of items, and in my work and theirs, a two-cluster solution has been used to identify high and low control individuals. There are two important problems with a cluster analysis approach. First, there is no operational definition of "clusters"; i.e., it is not possible for one researcher to use a specified set of criteria to replicate another's clusters with another sample. On occasion, I have addressed this problem by simply running my clusters against a coercive control scale and finding a cutting point that maximizes the fit between the cluster solution and a dichotomization of the scale.[9]

The second problem with cluster analysis is more serious. The nature of the clusters is heavily dependent on the nature of the sample. If the sample includes little or no intimate terrorism, as there is good reason to expect is the case for general survey samples, a cluster analysis on control tactics will still find a high and a low cluster, but the high cluster will not involve the level of coercion that is characteristic of intimate terrorism. Thus, I am not optimistic that cluster analyses of general survey samples can give us a very firm handle on the differences between intimate terrorism and situational couple violence. The so-called intimate terrorist group is likely to include a lot of situational couple violence and thus to comprise a larger portion of the violence in the sample than expected. In mixed samples, as with the Pittsburgh data, however, you're likely to have quite a few cases of situational couple violence from the general sample, and quite a few cases of intimate terrorism from the agency samples; thus, a cluster analysis is likely to give you a good representation of the types.

Here is the approach I would recommend for resolution of this dilemma. Take one of the standard measures of coercive control and administer it to a mixed sample that is likely to include a reasonable number of intimate terrorists. Do a cluster analysis to distinguish between intimate terrorism and situational couple violence. Then find the cutoff point on the control scale that best reproduces the clusters. Now, use that cutoff as the criterion for operationalizing intimate terrorism in other studies, and the first of those studies should be a mixed qualitative-quantitative study that assesses the validity of the operationalization with an agency sample. In that study, I would use both qualitative and quantitative data. For example, the cutoff would be validated quantitatively if it turned out to represent a point at which negative consequences for the victim, such as PTSD symptoms, jumped dramatically. But to tell you the truth, I have the most faith in a qualitative validation. Get the agency staff to provide their assessment of the type of violence involved in each case and see if that corresponds to the assignments done with the control scale.

What Is the Role of Violence in the Typology?

It is important that this typology is based entirely on the nonviolent coercive control that accompanies the violence. Every person in the typology is violent, but the frequency and severity of the violence has no bearing whatsoever on whether that violence is classified as intimate terrorism, violent resistance, situational couple violence, or mutual violent control. There are no items on physical violence in any of the control scales I use. Threats, yes; physical violence, no.

It is the combination of any level of violence with high coercive control that identifies intimate terrorism. Unlike Evan Stark, who includes the violence in his definition of "coercive control," I am not inclined to do so, although I agree completely with Stark that the violence is an essential part of the pattern I call "intimate terrorism." Control can be coercive without the presence of violence. It is the addition of the violence that adds the terror that gives intimate terrorism its name and its special horror.

The Data in this Book

I have used quite a variety of approaches to measuring coercive control because I work with secondary data sets collected by other researchers for other purposes. The disadvantage of this is that there is no way to construct strict comparisons of findings from one study with those of another. For example, there is no way to know whether there is more intimate terrorism in one sample than there is in another because the way intimate terrorism is identified is different in the different studies. The advantage of different operationalizations is that if one finds similar *patterns* from study to study, one can be confident that they are not an artifact of the way one measured his/her concepts. Indeed, that is what we have found. The basic differences between intimate terrorism and situational couple violence have been confirmed in studies using four different data sets, with different samples and different operationalizations of coercive control.

In the first section below, I provide complete sampling and measurement information for the analyses that were done specifically for this book. These were the data from the Pittsburgh or National Violence Against Women survey that I use without citation to a published or presented paper. After describing those data, I go on to describe the data sources used in papers on the typology that my colleagues and I have presented or published and that are cited frequently throughout the book.

SAMPLES AND MEASURES USED IN
THE ANALYSES FOR THIS BOOK

Pittsburgh Data. The Pittsburgh data come from 272 interviews with married or formerly married women living in southwestern Pennsylvania in the late 1970s. The nonrandom sampling design was a complex attempt to include a fairly large number of women in violent relationships, along with a comparison group of women in nonviolent relationships. Sampling began with three groups of women who had identified themselves as being in violent relationships: women who had visited a women's shelter, women who filed Protection from Abuse orders, and women who responded to flyers posted in laundromats, stores, and restrooms.[10] A comparison group was added by matching each battered woman to another married or formerly married woman from the same neighborhood.[11]

The Control Scale consisted of the following eleven items, culled from various parts of the interview: (1) "When you and your husband go places together, who decides where you will go?" (2) "If you disagree [about people you like], which people do the two of you spend more time with?" (3) "Does your husband know where you are when you are not together?" (4) "Are there places you might like to go but don't because you feel your husband wouldn't want you to? How often does this happen?" (5) "Do you generally do what your husband asks you to do?" (6) "Who decides how the family money will be spent in terms of major expenses?" (7) "[How often] does he try to get what he wants by doing any of the following: emotionally withdraws?" (8) "restricts your freedom?" (9) "stops having sex with you?" (10) "threatens to leave you?" (11) "Has your husband ever pressured you to have sexual relations?"

Alpha for the Control Scale is .76. Although that alpha is acceptable, I should point out that I am reluctant to even report alpha because one would not expect extremely high alphas for a control scale. Intimate terrorists will make use of the control tactics that are available to them and that work for them. The cutting point for high control was 2.74, placing 40 percent of the men and 10 percent of the women in the high control groups that were used to create the typology.

National Violence Against Women Survey (NVAWS). The NVAWS is a cross-sectional, national, random-sample telephone interview intended to examine several types of violence against women, including rape, physical assault, emotional abuse, and stalking.[12] Data were collected from a national, random-digit sample of telephone households in the United States; 8,005 men and 8,000 women, eighteen years of age or older, were interviewed. Because much of the published work dealing with partner violence focuses on married respondents and because other studies have shown differences in the nature of partner violence as a function of marital status, we chose to limit our analyses to the 4,967 women who were married at the time of the interview. The data we use refer to their current husbands. The NVAWS included seven items assessing nonviolent control tactics used by the respondent's husband. Many of these items were adopted from the Canadian Violence Against Women Survey[13] and closely resemble items included in the Psychological Maltreatment of Women Survey.[14] The items went like this: "Thinking about your current husband, would you say he . . ." (1) "is jealous or possessive?" (2) "tries to limit your contact with family and friends?" (3) "insists on knowing who you are with at all times?" (4) "calls you names or puts you down in front of others?" (5) makes you feel inadequate?" (6) "shouts or swears at you?" (7) "prevents you from knowing about or having access to the family income even when you ask?" Response options are simple: "Yes" or "No."

A principal components analysis was conducted to determine if the items represented more than one construct. The pattern of eigenvalues with a strong first factor (2.52, 1.06, .88, .71, .66, .59, and .58) suggested to us that a reasonable seven-item scale could be constructed from these items. The Control Scale score is the number of control tactics the respondent's husband was reported to have used, with a potential range of 0 to 7. The overall mean of the scale for all husbands is .39 (SD = .94), the median is 0, and actual scores cover the entire range from 0 to 7. Cronbach's alpha is .70.

To operationalize the distinction between intimate terrorism and situational couple violence, we needed to choose a cutting point to distinguish between high and low patterns of control. To avoid choosing a totally arbitrary cutting point, we used a cluster analysis of the seven individual items in the Control Scale to guide us. A k-means cluster analysis with a two-cluster solution was performed on the seven variables to identify natural clusters of controlling behavior for the violent husbands. We then chose our cutting point for the dichotomization to maximize the fit between the cluster solution and the dichotomized Control Scale. Husbands using three or more of the seven control tactics were coded *high control* (n = 211); those using two or fewer, as *low control* (n = 4,575). For researchers who may be using other measures of control, we point out that this cutting point corresponds to two standard deviations above the mean of the Control Scale for the reported behavior of all husbands in the NVAWS.

JOHNSON ET AL.: SIX OTHER PAPERS

The First Differential Effects Study. Early work with the Pittsburgh data (described above) used a different set of control items and relied entirely on a cluster analysis rather than simply dichotomizing a control scale.[15] Seven measures were created to tap control tactics analogous to those identified by Pence and Paymar: threats, economic control, use of privilege, using children, isolation, emotional abuse, and sexual control.[16]

Threats. Each measure of threats (one for husbands, the other for wives) is the mean of two items with five-point response formats ranging from "No, never" (1) to "Often" (5). The first item is: "Has your husband (Have you) ever gotten angry and *threatened* to use physical force with you (him)?" (Emphasis in survey instrument.) The second item followed a series of questions about violence directed at the spouse: "Is he (Are you) ever violent in other ways (such as throwing objects)?"

For wives' report of their husbands' behaviors, the mean of this variable is 2.72 (between "once" and "two or three times"); the standard deviation, 1.51; and the range, from 1.00 to 5.00. Cronbach's alpha for the two item scale is

.74. For wives' report of their own behaviors, the mean is 1.99 ("once"); the standard deviation, 1.05; the range, from 1.00 to 5.00; and alpha is .46.

Economic Control. Economic control is the average of two dichotomized items. The first asks, "Who decides how the family money will be spent in terms of major expenses?" It was dichotomized with a high score indicating that either "husband (wife) makes entire decision" or "husband (wife) has deciding vote." The second item asked for an open-ended response to "How much money do you (does your husband) have to spend during an average week without accounting to anyone?" The dichotomization cut-point was chosen to make this second item more an indicator of control than of disposable income: a response of $10 or less indicated high control, one of more than $10 indicated low control. For husbands' economic control, the two-item scale has a mean of 1.36, a standard deviation of .39, ranges from 1.00 to 2.00, and has an alpha of .46. For wives, the mean is 1.20; the standard deviation, .27; the range, from 1.00 to 2.00; and alpha is −.12.

Use of Privilege. This scale is the mean of six items, each of which indicates that the target person uses one of the following tactics to get his/her spouse to do what he/she wants. The six items were: (1) "suggests that you should do something because he knows best or because he feels he is an expert at a particular thing," (2) "restricts your freedom," (3) "stops having sex with you," (4) "threatens to leave you," (5) "emotionally withdraws," or (6) "suggest[s] that you should do something because other people do." The response format for all items addresses frequency, ranging from "Never" (1) to "Rarely" (3) to "Always" (5). For husbands, the scale has a mean of 2.03 ("Rarely"), a standard deviation of .81, ranges from 1.00 to 4.83, and an alpha of .76. For wives, the mean is 1.92 ("Rarely"), the standard deviation is .62, the range is from 1.00 to 4.19, and alpha is .65.

Using Children. There are three items in this data set that get at a spouse's use of the children to get his or her way with his/her partner. Two of them involve responses to the question, "When your husband is angry with you, how does he show it?" The two relevant response options were "Directs his anger to the children or pets" and "Uses physical violence with the children." The third item is "Does he ever try to get what he wants by doing any of the following to you? How often?" One of the actions listed is "Uses physical force against the kids to get what he wants from you," with the five response options ranging from "Never" to "Always." This item was dichotomized between "Never" and "Rarely," and the three items were averaged. For wives' report of their husbands' behaviors, the mean was 1.19; the standard deviation, .30; the range, from 1.00 to 2.00; and alpha, equal to .68. For wives' report of their own behaviors, the mean was 1.12; standard deviation, .21; the range, from 1.00 to 2.00; and alpha, equal to .41.

Isolation. The measure of isolation is the mean of two items with five-point response formats ranging from "Never" to "Always." The items are: (1) "Does your husband know where you are when you are not together?" and (2) "Are there places you might like to go but don't because you feel your husband wouldn't want you to? How often does this happen?" For wives' reports of their husbands' behaviors, the mean of this measure is 3.32 (between "sometimes" and "usually"), the standard deviation is .77, the observed range is from 1.00 to 5.00, and alpha is equal to .09. For wives' reports of their own behaviors, the mean is 2.64 (between "rarely" and "sometimes"), the standard deviation is .84, the range is from 1.00 to 5.00, and alpha equals .06.

Emotional Abuse. The three-item emotional abuse scale includes one item that gets at active abuse (sex is sometimes unpleasant because "He compares you unfavorably to other women "), and two "passive abuse" items that indicate that he never or rarely praises, and never or rarely is "nice to you in other ways (smiling, concerned with how you are feeling, calling you affectionate names, etc.)." All three items are dichotomies. For husbands the mean is 1.25, the standard deviation is .33, the scale ranges from 1.00 to 2.00, and alpha is .57. For wives the mean is 1.08, the standard deviation is .21, the range is from 1.00 to 2.00, and alpha is .48.

Sexual Control. There are two items in the sexual control scale, tapping whether sex is ever unpleasant because "he forces me to have sex when I don't want to," or "he makes you do things you don't want to do." Both items are dichotomies. For husbands the mean is 1.22, the standard deviation .36, the range is from 1.00 to 2.00, and alpha is .70. For wives the mean 1.02, the standard deviation is .01, the range is 1.00 to 2.00, and alpha is .35.

A violent respondent was identified by the wife's responses to two questions about violence, one referring to her, the other to her husband, each embedded in a section of the interview concerning anger. Although the specific question does not mention anger, it follows a series of fifteen questions about how she and her husband show their anger. The specific question was: "Has he (Have you) ever actually slapped or pushed you (him) or used other physical force with you (him)?" The five-point response format included "No, never," "Once," "Two or three times," "Several times," and "Often." It was dichotomized between "No, never" and the other responses, to distinguish ever-violent from nonviolent individuals.

The clustering algorithm was Ward's method, an agglomerative approach that selects each new case to add to a cluster on the basis of its effect on the overall homogeneity of the cluster, and which therefore tends to produce tightly defined clusters, rather than strings. Each of the control tactic indices was standardized, and Euclidean distance was the measure of dissimilarity. The index of dissimilarity gradually increases up to a major jump immediately prior to the two-cluster solution. The "meaning" of the two clusters can be adduced from a look at the average profile for the members of the two clusters. The pattern is quite simple, with one cluster (High Control) simply being high on all of the seven control tactics relative to the second cluster. Looking at the standardized scores, we see that the High Control cluster is on average roughly one standard deviation or more above the mean for every one of the seven nonviolent control tactics.

The Second Differential Effects Study. These are the data described above as the Pittsburgh data.[17]

The Third Differential Effects Study. These data are described above as the National Violence Against Women Survey data.[18]

The Fourth Differential Effects Study. The data come from the Effects of Violence on Work and Family Study,[19] a cross-sectional study conducted to examine the association between low-income, ethnic minority women's labor force participation and their experiences of partner violence.[20] Participants were a random sample of 824 women, 18 years or older, who lived in Humboldt Park, a low-income neighborhood in Chicago. The sampling frame consisted of the total number of housing units by block and census tract in the community area, which contained 299 blocks with a mean number of 57 housing units per block. Humboldt Park was chosen primarily because of its relatively equal distribution of African Americans (51 percent) and Hispanics (43 percent). Data were collected over an eight-month period, September 1994 through April 1995, yielding an overall response rate of 54 percent. Households were randomly selected to participate in the study, and recruitment consisted of up to five attempts to screen each household. There were 642 instances in which a screening instrument could not be administered because no one answered the door. It can be assumed that 85 percent of these women would have been eligible for the survey, yielding an additional 546 of the "eligible respondents" who were nonresponsive. The 54 percent response rate was calculated as the total number of completed interviews (n = 824) divided by the total number of respondents known to be eligible (n = 989) plus the total number of respondents assumed to be eligible (n = 546). Had the 546 cases been excluded from this ratio, a response rate of 83 percent would have been obtained. Interviews took place within the women's homes and were conducted by female interviewers in either Spanish or English, depending on the preference of the respondent. Finally, questionnaires were read aloud by the interviewers so that all women could participate regardless of literacy skills and, whenever possible, interviewers were matched with respondents in terms of language, race, and ethnicity.

Respondents who were not currently in an intimate relationship with a man (n = 187), did not answer all of the violence or control questions described below (n = 41), or were not of Hispanic or black origin (n = 41) were excluded from our analyses, yielding a sample of 563 women in the current study (these numbers do not add up to 824 because a woman may have been characterized by more than one exclusionary criterion). Respondents who were currently married but separated from their spouses at the time of the study were included in the analyses because partner violence often continues even after women escape or end a violent relationship.

Respondents represent a relatively low-resource population. Nearly half of the respondents had not completed high school or earned a GED and more than half reported that they were unemployed at the time of the survey. Further, respondents reported that there were, on average, four people residing in the household, two of whom were children. According to the U.S. Census Bureau, the 1994 poverty threshold for a household with these demographics was $15,029. The median household income for the women in this study, therefore, was slightly above the poverty threshold. However, only 37 percent of respondents answered this question—61 percent reported not knowing their household income and 2 percent refused to provide this information. Finally, about one-third of the respondents received Aid to Families with Dependent Children and slightly less than half received food stamps.

Physical violence was assessed by means of a modified version of the Conflict Tactics Scales.[21] Respondents answered the following ten questions: (1) "In the past 12 months, when you've had an argument, how often did your husband/boyfriend throw something at you?" (2) "push, grab, or shove you?" (3) "slap you?" (4) "kick, bite, or hit you with his fists?" (5) "hit or try to hit you with an object?" (6) "beat you up?" (7) "choke you?" (8) "force you to have sex or do sexual things you didn't want to do?" (9) "burn you?" or (10) "cut you with a knife or fire a gun at you?" Responses ranged from "Never" (1) to "Very Often" (5). The Physical Violence Scale was the mean of responses to the ten violence items (Cronbach's alpha = .85). This scale combines both the *severity* and the *frequency* in which each form of violence was used and therefore reflects women's overall experiences of physical violence. Respondents who reported "Never" on all of the physical violence items (n = 452) were coded as "Non-Violent"; all others (n = 111) were coded as "Experienced Violence."

Two control tactics scales were constructed from the following eight items: (1) "In the past 12 months, when you've had an argument, how often did your husband/boyfriend insult you, swear at you, or call you out of your name?" (2) "accuse you of being with another man?" (3) "do or say something just to spite you?" (4) "try to control your every move?" (5) "withhold money, make you ask for money, or take yours?" (6) "threaten you with a knife or gun?" (7) "threaten to kill you?" or (8) "threaten to hurt your family or friends?" Responses for all items ranged from "Never" (1) to "Very Often" (5). An exploratory principal components factor analysis suggested that the items loaded onto two factors. Factor 1 (eigenvalue = 3.34) consisted of items representing verbally aggressive, coercive, and degrading behavior toward the women (e.g., "accuse you of being with another man?" "withhold money, make you ask for money, or take yours?"). We called this factor "Verbal Abuse and Coercion" (Cronbach's alpha = .78). Factor 2 (eigenvalue = 1.39) included items representing the threat of violence against the women or against the women's family or friends (e.g., "threaten to kill you?" "threaten to hurt your family or friends?"). We called this factor "Threats" (Cronbach's alpha = .68).

Results of a Ward's method cluster analysis indicated that a three-cluster solution was optimal for these data. Our decision concerning the number of clusters was based both on theory and assessment of changes in the average squared Euclidean distance within clusters as the clusters were combined. The index of dissimilarity exhibited a large increase between the three- and two-cluster solutions. Cluster 1 (n = 19) was a high control cluster: respondents reported high levels on both Verbal Abuse and Coercion (M = 3.49, SD = .69) and Threats (M = 2.39, SD = .69). Cluster 2 (n = 35) was a specific type of control: respondents reported high levels on Verbal Abuse and Coercion (M = 3.02, SD = .40), but not Threats (M = 1.00, SD = .00). Cluster 3 (n = 57) was a low control cluster, with respondents reporting low levels on both Verbal Abuse and Coercion (M = 1.62, SD = .40) and Threats (M = 1.03, SD = .13). We labeled Cluster 1 "Intimate Terrorism," Cluster 2 "Control/No Threat," and Cluster 3 "Situational Couple Violence."

The Help-Seeking Study. Data for the help-seeking study came from the Chicago Women's Health Risk Study (CWHRS),[22] a cross-sectional study conducted to identify significant factors associated with partner-perpetrated life-threatening injury or death.[23] CWHRS targeted specific neighborhoods in the Chicago area that, based on the Chicago Homicide Dataset, had high rates of lethal intimate violence relative to other Chicago areas. Data were collected between June 1997 and April 1998.

To minimize selection bias, the CWHRS employed a universal screening design, intended to screen all female trauma and walk-in patients for partner violence. The instrument used to screen respondents for partner violence was based on the Intimate Violence Screening Tool, developed by the Chicago Department of Health.[24] This screening process was instituted into the standard intake procedure for all women receiving treatment in the health care setting. A sample of 2,616 female trauma and walk-in patients who entered one of three Chicago health care clinics/hospitals was screened. Patients were asked the following three questions: (1) "Has your intimate partner ever hit, slapped, kicked or otherwise physically hurt or threatened you?" (2) "Has your intimate partner ever forced you to engage in sexual activities that made you feel uncomfortable?" and (3) "Are you afraid of your intimate partner?" Respondents who answered "Yes" to any of the three screening questions, were in a current intimate relationship, and were eighteen years or older were screened as "Abused" by the staff conducting the screening. Women who answered "No" to all of the questions or who experienced abuse more than one year prior to the screening were screened as "Not abused."

Screening results were available for 2,177 women (524 "Abused" and 1,653 "Not Abused" women). The CWHRS sample design called for interviewing all women screened as "Abused" and 40 percent of the women screened as "Not Abused." Approximately 86 percent (n = 497) of the "Abused" women and 31 percent (n = 208) of the "Not Abused" women were actually interviewed, totaling 705 women.

The sample for our study consisted of a subgroup of the 497 "Abused" women. Respondents who met the following four criteria were included in the current study: Respondents reported that (1) they experienced at least one incident of physical violence in the twelve months prior to the survey (n = 479, 96 percent); (2) all incidents of physical violence were committed by the same intimate partner (n = 456, 92 percent); and (3) the intimate partner was male (n = 475, 96 percent). Finally, women needed to have (4) answered all questions regarding experiences of nonviolent power and control tactics (n = 434, 87 percent). These four criteria yielded a sample of 389 women.

Violence type was defined by responses to five dichotomous (0 = No; 1 = Yes) questions, which make up the Power and Control Scale: (1) "In the past year, an intimate partner was jealous and didn't want you to talk to another man," (2) "tried to limit your contact with family or friends," (3) "insisted on knowing who you are with and where you are at all times," (4) "called you names to put you down or made you feel bad," and (5) "prevented you from knowing or having access to family income, even if you asked."

A Ward's Method cluster analysis of the Power and Control Scale was used to classify partner violence as either intimate terrorism or situational couple violence. Cluster 1 represents a less controlling group, with respondents reporting fewer than five types of control. We labeled this cluster "Situational Couple Violence." Cluster 2 represents a highly controlling group, with respondents reporting all five types of control. We labeled this cluster "Intimate Terrorism."

Appendix B
Stalking and
Separation-Precipitated
Violence

To tell the truth, I simply didn't know where to put this material; it "belongs" in the chapters on intimate terrorism, on violent resistance, and on situational couple violence. Much postseparation violence and stalking are essentially a continuation of intimate terrorism after the abuser has lost the easy access afforded by living with his victim; so I could have put this material into chapter 2, on intimate terrorism. However, the other side of the intimate terrorism coin is the victim; it has long been recognized that the most dangerous time for victims of intimate terrorism is when they try to leave their abuser, because of the possibility of increased violence and/or stalking after the separation Thus, I could have placed this material in the section on leaving in chapter 3, on violent resistance. Finally, there is another type of separation-precipitated violence that has been a topic of interest in the divorce literature for decades, and that may be more like situational couple violence than intimate terrorism. This is violence in a relationship that has had no history of violence until the conflicts raised by the separation escalate to violence; I therefore could have placed this discussion in chapter 4, on situational couple violence. Given that the issues seemed to belong in three different places in the book, and were not central to any of them, it seemed the best tactic was simply to put this discussion into an appendix and refer to it in each of those chapters where appropriate.

Intimate Terrorism and the Risks of Leaving

The feminist analysis of domestic violence has long recognized that attempting to leave an intimate terrorist puts a woman at increased risk of violence at his hands, because leaving is the ultimate threat to his control. Early research showed that, contrary to common belief, the majority of women who were victims of intimate partner assault were separated or divorced.[1] Another government report indicated that women separated from their husbands were twenty-five times more likely than married women to be assaulted by their partners.[2] And the postseparation violence can be homicidal. A recent eleven-city study comparing cases in which women had been murdered by their partners with a control group of abused women found that among the major risk factors for homicide was "estrangement, especially from a controlling partner."[3] Similarly, a Canadian study found that the risk of being killed by their intimate partner is almost ten times greater for women separated from their husbands than for those still married.[4] Attempts to retain or regain control after a partner leaves often go beyond the use of violence, involving many of the same tactics that were used within the relationship to monitor and control the partner before she left. Of course, such behavior is most familiar to us as "stalking"; a recent comprehensive review of the stalking literature indicates that half of all stalking emerges from preexisting romantic relationships.[5] Ending the relationship does not always end the abuse.

Separation-Precipitated Violence
That May Be Situational Couple Violence

In 1993, Johnston and Campbell published a landmark study of 140 high-conflict divorcing families, in which they distinguish among five different types of partner violence.[6] The one of most interest to me here is what they call "violence engendered by separation or postdivorce trauma." The critical distinguishing feature of these cases is that there had been no violence prior to the beginning of the separation process; violence in these types of cases has come to be identified as "separation-engendered" in the divorce literature. Because there had been no prior history of violence, one might assume that these cases all involve situational couple violence. However, there are two other possibilities. First, in some cases one of the partners (almost all of these cases involve violent men) may already have been what I refer to in chapter 2 as an "incipient intimate terrorist," engaging in a wide range of tactics of coercive control but no violence—yet. The threat to his control posed by the separation process leads him to escalate his control tactics to include violence. The second possibility is intimate terrorism that is precipitated entirely by the separation process. In this case, the violent partner has not been controlling until faced with the loss of his partner, but he now begins to engage in a range of control tactics, including violence.

The general point to be made here is that postseparation violence could be any of the types of violence discussed in this book. As with other intimate partner violence, if human service agencies want to make informed decisions about the services that would best meet the needs of the victim and other members of her family, they will need to learn more about the nature of the relationship in which the violence is embedded.

Appendix C

Gender and Intimate Partner Violence

Let me begin with a reminder that in heterosexual relationships the strongest correlate of type of intimate partner violence is gender. Intimate terrorism is perpetrated almost entirely by men, and the violent resistance to it is from their female partners. The gendering of situational couple violence is less clear, but men and women are roughly equally likely to report that they were involved in situational couple violence.

Gender and Intimate Terrorism

To a sociologist, the tremendous gender imbalance in the perpetration of intimate terrorism suggests important social structural causes that go beyond simple differences between men and women. Understanding the role of gender in intimate partner violence requires the application of the theoretical framework that has come to be known as "gender theory."[1] For over two decades now, feminist sociologists have argued that gender must be understood as an institution, not merely an individual characteristic. Although some gender theorists have couched this argument in terms of rejecting gender as an individual characteristic in favor of focusing at the situational or institutional level of analysis, I prefer a version of gender theory that incorporates gender at all levels of social organization, from the individual level of gender differences in identities and attitudes and even physical differences, through the situational enforcement of gender in social interaction, to the gender structure of organizational and societal contexts.[2] The application of gender theory to intimate terrorism in the following paragraphs will begin with individual sex differences and work up to the gender structure of the economy, the family, and the criminal justice system.

Why is intimate terrorism (and violent resistance to it) so clearly a matter of men abusing women in heterosexual relationships? First, gender (or in this case, biological sex) affects the use of violence to control one's partner in heterosexual relationships simply because of average sex differences in size and strength. The use of violence as one tactic in an attempt to exercise general control over one's partner requires more than the willingness to do violence. It requires a credible threat of a damaging, violent response to noncompliance. Such a threat is, of course, more credible coming from a man than a woman simply because of the size difference in most heterosexual couples. Furthermore, still at the level of individual differences but focusing on gender socialization rather than physical differences, experience with violence and individual attitudes toward violence both make such threats more likely and more credible from a man than from a woman. Put simply, the exercise of violence is more likely to be a part of boys' and men's experience than girls' and women's—in sports, fantasy play, and real-life conflict.

Second, individual misogyny and gender traditionalism are clearly implicated in intimate terrorism. Although critics of feminist theory often claim that there is no relationship between domestic violence and attitudes toward women, the research that has addressed this question in fact clearly supports the position that individual men's attitudes toward women affect the likelihood that they will be involved in intimate terrorism. One example is Amy Holtzworth-Munroe's work, which shows that both of her two groups of intimate terrorists are more hostile toward women than are either nonviolent men or men involved in situational couple violence.[3] More generally, Sugarman and Frankel conducted a thorough review of the research on this question, using a statistical technique that allowed them to combine the findings of all of the studies that had been published up to that time.[4] While Holtzworth-Munroe demonstrated an effect of hostility toward women, Sugarman and Frankel focused on the effects of men's attitudes toward the role of women in social life, and found that traditional men were more likely to be involved in attacks on their partners than were nontraditional men. Some of the details of the Sugarman and Frankel review provide further support for the important role of attitudes toward women in intimate terrorism. They found that men's attitudes toward women were much more strongly related to violence in studies using samples that were dominated by intimate terrorism than in studies that were dominated by situational couple violence. Of course, this is exactly what a feminist theory of domestic violence would predict. It is intimate terrorism that involves the attempt to control one's partner, an undertaking supported by traditional or hostile attitudes toward women.

Third, at the level of social interaction rather than individual attitudes, our cultures of masculinity and femininity ensure that whatever the level of violence, its meaning will differ greatly depending upon the gender of the perpe-

trator.[5] When a woman slaps her husband in the heat of an argument, it is unlikely to be interpreted by him as a serious attempt to do him physical harm.
In fact, it is likely to be seen as a quaint form of feminine communication.
Women's violence is taken less seriously, is less likely to produce fear, and is
therefore less likely either to be intended as a control tactic or to be successful
as one.[6]

Fourth, general social norms regarding intimate heterosexual partnerships,
although certainly in the midst of considerable historical change, are heavily
gendered and rooted in a patriarchal heterosexual model that validates men's
power.[7] These norms affect the internal functioning of all relationships, regardless of the individual attitudes of the partners, because couples' social
networks are often involved in shaping the internal workings of personal relationships.[8] When those networks support a male-dominant style of marriage
or a view of marriage as a commitment "for better or worse," they can contribute to the entrapment of women in abusive relationships.

Finally, the gendering of the broader social context within which the relationship is embedded affects the resources the partners can draw upon to shape
the relationship and to cope with or escape from the violence. For example,
the gender gap in wages can create an economic dependency that enhances
men's control over women and contributes to women's entrapment in abusive
relationships. The societal assignment of caregiving responsibilities primarily
to women further contributes to this economic dependency, placing women
in a subordinate position within the family, and creating a context in which institutions (such as the church) that could be a source of support for abused
women, instead encourage them to stay in abusive relationships—for the sake
of the children or for the sake of the marriage. Then there is the criminal justice system, heavily dominated by men, and involving a culture of masculinity
that has not always been responsive to the problems of women experiencing
intimate terrorism, which was often treated as if it were situational couple violence.[9] On a more positive note, there have been major changes in all of these
systems as a result of the women's movement in general, and the battered
women's movement in particular.[10] These changes are probably a major source
of the recent dramatic decline in nonfatal intimate partner violence against
women and fatal intimate partner violence against men in the United States.[11]

What About Situational Couple Violence?

It is not surprising that the institution of gender, in which male domination is a central element, is implicated in the structure of intimate terrorism,

which is about coercive control. In contrast, situational couple violence, which is the most common type of partner violence, does not involve an attempt on the part of one partner to gain general control over the other, and by some criteria it appears to be more gender-symmetric. The violence is situationally provoked, as the tensions or emotions of a particular encounter lead one or both of the partners to resort to violence. Intimate relationships inevitably involve conflicts, and in some relationships one or more of those conflicts turns into an argument that escalates into violence. The violence may be minor and singular, or the violence could be a chronic problem, with one or both partners frequently resorting to violence, minor or severe, even homicidal. In general, there is considerable variability in the nature of situational couple violence, a variability that has not yet been explored adequately enough to allow us to make confident statements about its causes.

Nevertheless, some researchers *have* made confident statements about one aspect of situational couple violence: its gender symmetry—a symmetry that in my view is mythical. This myth of gender symmetry has been supported by the widespread use of a particularly meaningless measure of symmetry—prevalence. Respondents in a survey are presented with a list of violent behaviors ranging from a push or a slap to an attack with a weapon. They are then asked to report how often they have committed each violent act against their partner (or their partner against them) in the previous twelve months. "Prevalence of partner violence" is then defined as the percentage of a group (e.g., men or women) who have committed the act (or some set of the acts, often identified as mild or severe violent acts) at least once in the previous twelve months. The much-touted gender symmetry of situational couple violence is gender symmetry only in this narrow sense. For example, in the 1975 National Survey of Family Violence that initiated the gender symmetry debate, 13 percent of women and 11 percent of men had committed at least one of the acts listed in the Conflict Tactics Scales.[12] However, by any sensible measure of the nature of the violence—such as the specific acts engaged in, the injuries produced, the frequency of the violence, or the production of fear in one's partner—intimate partner violence (even situational couple violence) is not gender-symmetric.[13] Thus, although situational couple violence may not be as gendered as intimate terrorism and violent resistance, many of the gender factors discussed above are implicated in the patterning of situational couple violence. For instance, in situational couple violence, the likelihood of injury or fear is influenced by size differences: a slap from a woman is still perceived as an entirely different act than is one from a man. Most importantly, our cultures of masculinity and femininity contribute to the couple communication problems that are often associated with situational couple violence.[14]

A Note on Same-Sex Relationships

It is important to note that this discussion of gender and intimate partner violence is relevant only to heterosexual relationships. In same-sex relationships, some aspects of gender may still be important (e.g., gender differences in attitudes toward and experience with violence might produce more violence in gay men's relationships than in lesbian relationships), others will be largely irrelevant (e.g., gay and lesbian relationship norms are more egalitarian, and sex differences in size and strength will be less likely to be significant), and some will play themselves out in quite different ways (e.g., reactions of the criminal justice system may be affected by officers' attitudes toward gay men and lesbians). Although we know considerably less about same-sex relationships than we do about heterosexual relationships, there is a growing literature that is important not only in its own right, but also because it sheds light on some of the inadequacies of theories rooted in research on heterosexual relationships.[15]

Notes

Introduction (pages 1–4)

1. Catherine Kirkwood, *Leaving Abusive Partners: From the Scars of Survival to the Wisdom for Change* (Newbury Park, Calif: Sage, 1993), 44.

2. There are some important terminological issues involved in discussions of the problem of intimate partner violence. I will use such terms as "intimate partner violence" and "partner violence" when I want to refer broadly to any violence in any sort of intimate partner relationship, including marriage, dating relationships, cohabiting relationships, and same-sex as well as opposite-sex relationships. I will use the terms "battering," "partner abuse," "spouse abuse," and "wife-beating" pretty much interchangeably—and which I will label later as "intimate terrorism"—to refer to the sort of pattern described in the epigram to this introduction. This is violence that is embedded in a general pattern of both violent and nonviolent controlling behavior.

3. Michael P. Johnson, "Patriarchal Terrorism and Common Couple Violence: Two Forms of Violence against Women," *Journal of Marriage and the Family* 57, no. 2 (1995).

4. Evan Stark and Anne Flitcraft, *Women at Risk: Domestic Violence and Women's Health* (Thousand Oaks, Calif.: Sage, 1996).

5. James Alan Fox and Marianne W. Zawitz, "Homicide Trends in the United States," (Bureau of Justice Statistics, U.S. Department of Justice, June 29, 2006 [accessed July 6, 2007]); available from http://www.ojp.usdoj.gov/bjs/homicide/homtrnd .htm. This number has been steadily declining in recent years, from 1,571 in 1993 to 1,159 in 2004, probably due to the changes brought about through the efforts of the battered women's movement. See also figure 3, p. 58.

6. R. Emerson Dobash and Russell P. Dobash, *Women, Violence and Social Change* (New York: Routledge, 1992), 251–84.

7. Ellen Pence and Michael Paymar, *Education Groups for Men Who Batter: The Duluth Model* (New York: Springer, 1993).

8. Demie Kurz, "Social Science Perspectives on Wife Abuse: Current Debates and Future Directions," *Gender & Society* 3, no. 4 (1989).

9. Rancorous as this debate has been within academia, where debates are usually somewhat staid, the level of vitriol is much higher in the public politics of domestic violence, where the two sides of the gender debate openly accuse each other of purposeful, gross distortions of the evidence to support their various positions. For example, see the men's rights attacks on feminist perspectives on domestic violence at http://www.mediaradar.org/.

10. Johnson, "Patriarchal Terrorism and Common Couple Violence."

11. Jana L. Jasinski and Linda M. Williams, eds., *Partner Violence: A Comprehensive Review of 20 Years of Research* (Thousand Oaks, Calif.: Sage, 1998).

Chapter 1. Control and Violence in Intimate Relationships (pages 5–24)

1. R. Emerson Dobash and Russell P. Dobash, *Violence against Wives: A Case against Patriarchy* (New York: Free Press, 1979), 94.

2. I have avoided using the term "perpetrator" here because it implies that the violent resister is the primary initiator of the violence in the relationship. That certainly is not the case for violent resistance. A violent resister is, however, a perpetrator in the sense of having committed a violent act, and should that violence come to the attention of the criminal justice system, "perpetrator" is the term that would be applied.

3. Ellen Pence and Michael Paymar, *Education Groups for Men Who Batter: The Duluth Model* (New York: Springer, 1993).

4. I am going to use gendered pronouns here because, as I will show later, the vast majority of intimate terrorists are men terrorizing female partners. That does not mean that women are never intimate terrorists. There are a small number of women who do terrorize their male partners, and there are also women in same-sex relationships who terrorize their partners. I will discuss both of these situations later. Suzanne K. Steinmetz, "The Battered Husband Syndrome," *Victimology* 2, no. 3-sup-4 (1977–78): Claire M. Renzetti, *Violent Betrayal: Partner Abuse in Lesbian Relationships* (Thousand Oaks, Calif.: Sage, 1992).

5. Catherine Kirkwood, *Leaving Abusive Partners: From the Scars of Survival to the Wisdom for Change* (Newbury Park, Calif.: Sage, 1993).

6. Once again, I will use gendered pronouns because most violent resisters are women in heterosexual relationships. There certainly are also violent resisters in same-sex relationships and in the small number of cases in which a woman is able to terrorize her male partner.

7. Lenore E. Walker, "Legal Self-Defense for Battered Women," in *Battering and Family Therapy: A Feminist Perspective*, ed. Marsali Hansen and Michele Harway (Thousand Oaks, Calif.: Sage, 1993); Lenore E. Walker, *Terrifying Love: Why Battered Women Kill and How Society Responds* (New York: Harper & Row, 1989).

8. Linda L. Ammons, "Dealing with the Nastiness: Mixing Feminism and Criminal Law in the Review of Cases of Battered Incarcerated Women—a Tenth-Year Reflection," *Buffalo Criminal Law Review* 4 (2001).

9. I am not going to go into great detail about how social scientists ask questions about violence. The most common approach has been to ask separate questions about each of a series of specific violent acts, such as "Have you ever pushed, slapped, or shoved your partner?" or "Have you ever attacked your partner with a knife or a gun?" This approach has the virtue of not leaving the definition of violence up to the respondent and of helping to jog the respondent's memory by asking about specific acts. The most commonly used set of such questions is part of the Conflict Tactics

Scales developed by Murray Straus and his colleagues. It has been used in hundreds of studies of partner violence. Murray A. Straus, "The Conflict Tactics Scales and Its Critics: An Evaluation and New Data on Validity and Reliability," in *Physical Violence in American Families: Risk Factors and Adaptations to Violence in 8,145 Families*, ed. Murray A. Straus and Richard J. Gelles (New Brunswick, N.J.: Transaction Press, 1990); Murray A. Straus, "Measuring Intrafamily Conflict and Violence: The Conflict Tactics (CT) Scales," in *Physical Violence in American Families*; Murray A. Straus et al., "The Revised Conflict Tactics Scales (CTS2): Development and Preliminary Psychometric Data," *Journal of Family Issues* 17, no. 3 (1996). The CTS has not been immune to criticism. R. Emerson Dobash and Russell P. Dobash, *Women, Violence and Social Change* (New York: Routledge, 1992), 274–81.

10. This is the principle of "equifinality" in motivational research: if a variety of an organism's behaviors all lead to the same end, one can infer a motive. This approach to motivation is essential in work with animals that cannot report their motives to us, but it is equally useful with humans who may miscommunicate their motives or not even recognize them.

11. Lonnie H. Athens, *Violent Criminal Acts and Actors Revisited* (Chicago: University of Illinois Press, 1997); Richard B. Felson and Steven F. Messner, "The Control Motive in Intimate Partner Violence," *Social Psychology Quarterly* 63, no. 1 (2000).

12. Harold H. Kelley et al., *Close Relationships* (New York: W. H. Freeman, 1983).

13. Until the 1990s almost all of this work had been focused on heterosexual relationships. Recently, we have begun to learn more about patterns of power and control in same-sex relationships. Beth Leventhal and Sandra E. Lundy, eds., *Same-Sex Domestic Violence: Strategies for Change* (Thousand Oaks, Calif.: Sage, 1999); Renzetti, *Violent Betrayal*; Claire M. Renzetti and Charles Harvey Miley, *Violence in Gay and Lesbian Domestic Partnerships* (New York: Haworth Press, 1996). In many ways, they are similar to those found in heterosexual relationships; in some ways, different. For example, threat of "outing" is a control tactic that is available to some abusive gay or lesbian partners.

14. Dobash and Dobash, *Violence against Wives*; Lenore E. Walker, *The Battered Woman* (New York: Harper & Row, 1979).

15. Dobash and Dobash, *Violence against Wives*.

16. Diana E. Russell, *Rape in Marriage* (New York: Collier Books, 1982).

17. Pence and Paymar, *The Duluth Model*.

18. Mary Ann Dutton and Lisa A. Goodman, "Coercion in Intimate Partner Violence: Toward a New Conceptualization," *Sex Roles* 52, no. 11/12 (2005); Evan Stark, *Coercive Control: The Entrapment of Women in Personal Life* (New York: Oxford University Press, 2007).

19. Mary Ann Dutton and Lisa A. Goodman, May 2002. Personal communication.

20. Jan E. Stets, *Domestic Violence and Control* (New York: Springer-Verlag, 1988).

21. Deeana L. Jang, Leni Martin, and Gail Pendleton, *Domestic Violence in Immigrant and Refugee Communities: Asserting the Rights of Battered Women* (Washington, D.C.: Family Violence Prevention Fund, 1997).

22. Valerie Nash Chang, *I Just Lost Myself: Psychological Abuse of Women in Marriage* (Westport, Conn.: Praeger, 1996); K. Daniel O'Leary and Roland D. Maiuro, eds., *Psychological Abuse in Violent Domestic Relations* (New York: Springer, 2001); Richard M. Tolman, "Psychological Abuse of Women," in *Assessment of Family Violence: A Clinical and Legal Sourcebook*, ed. Robert T. Ammerman and Michel Hersen (New York: John Wiley, 1992).

23. Susan Lloyd and Nina Taluc, "The Effects of Male Violence on Female Employment," *Violence Against Women* 5, no. 4 (1999).

24. Steinmetz, "The Battered Husband Syndrome."

25. Elizabeth Pleck et al., "The Battered Data Syndrome: A Comment on Steinmetz' Article," *Victimology* 2 (1978).

26. Russell P. Dobash et al., "The Myth of Sexual Symmetry in Marital Violence," *Social Problems* 39, no. 1 (1992).

27. John Archer, "Sex Differences in Aggression between Heterosexual Partners: A Meta-Analytic Review," *Psychological Bulletin* 126, no. 5 (2000).

28. I use the word "groups" here loosely. Although some of the scholars within each group have collaborated with each other, these groups are identified primarily by the theoretical frameworks that drive their work and the sources from which they generally gather their information. Michael P. Johnson, "Patriarchal Terrorism and Common Couple Violence: Two Forms of Violence against Women," *Journal of Marriage and the Family* 57, no. 2 (1995); Demie Kurz, "Social Science Perspectives on Wife Abuse: Current Debates and Future Directions," *Gender & Society* 3, no. 4 (1989): 489–505.

29. Richard J. Gelles, "Violence in the Family: A Review of Research in the Seventies," *Journal of Marriage & the Family* 42, no. 4 (1980); Murray A. Straus, "A General Systems Theory Approach to a Theory of Violence between Family Members," *Social Science Information* 12, no. 3 (1973); Murray A. Straus, Richard J. Gelles, and Suzanne K. Steinmetz, *Behind Closed Doors: Violence in the American Family* (Garden City, N.Y.: Doubleday, 1980).

30. Dobash and Dobash, *Violence against Wives*; Dell Martin, *Battered Wives* (New York: Pocket Books, 1976); Mildred Daley Pagelow, *Woman-Battering: Victims and Their Experiences* (Newbury Park, Calif.: Sage, 1981); Maria Roy, ed., *Battered Women: A Psychosociological Study of Domestic Violence* (New York: Van Nostrand Reinhold, 1977); Walker, *The Battered Woman*.

31. Johnson, "Patriarchal Terrorism and Common Couple Violence."

32. Murray A. Straus, "Injury and Frequency of Assault and the 'Representative Sample Fallacy' in Measuring Wife Beating and Child Abuse," in *Physical Violence in American Families*.

33. Johnson, "Patriarchal Terrorism and Common Couple Violence."

34. Much of the gender debate in the literature has centered on the inadequacies of these questions, called the Conflict Tactics Scales or CTS, as a means to assess partner violence. Dobash et al., "The Myth of Sexual Symmetry in Marital Violence"; Straus, "The Conflict Tactics Scales." Whatever the inadequacies of the CTS may be, it

is the most widely used instrument for assessing level of partner violence. Comparing studies that all used the CTS eliminated this potential source of bias.

35. Dobash and Dobash, *Violence against Wives*; Pence and Paymar, *The Duluth Model*; Evan Stark and Anne Flitcraft, *Women at Risk: Domestic Violence and Women's Health* (Thousand Oaks, Calif.: Sage, 1996).

36. The terminology I use has changed somewhat over the years, although the definitions have remained the same. My 1995 paper refers to "patriarchal terrorism" and "common couple violence." I soon abandoned the former term because it begs the question of men's and women's relative involvement in this form of controlling violence. It also implies that all such intimate terrorism is somehow rooted in patriarchal structures, traditions, or attitudes. I still believe that intimate terrorism is perpetrated primarily by men in heterosexual relationships and that in such cases the violence is, indeed, rooted in patriarchal traditions. However, it is clear that there are women who are intimate terrorists in both heterosexual and same-sex relationships. Renzetti, *Violent Betrayal*. Furthermore, it is not necessarily the case that all intimate terrorism, even men's, is rooted in patriarchal ideas or structures. With regard to "common couple violence," I abandoned it in favor of "situational couple violence" because the former terminology implies to some readers that I feel that such violence is acceptable. I also prefer the new terminology because it more clearly identifies the roots of this violence in the situated escalation of conflict.

37. Methodological details of the data on which I rely most heavily in this book are included in appendix A, along with a general discussion of some of the major issues involved in identifying the different types of intimate partner violence.

38. Jan E. Stets and Murray A. Straus, "Gender Differences in Reporting Marital Violence and Its Medical and Psychological Consequences," in *Physical Violence in American Families.*

39. It is also possible that there is a measurement error issue involved in this finding. The difference between situational couple violence (SCV) and intimate terrorism (IT) amounts to being on one side or the other of a cutoff between "low" and "high" on the Coercive Control Scale. The choice of cutoff is somewhat arbitrary, and there are likely to be some low-control cases that may actually involve intimate terrorism. This is one of those areas in social science where I am convinced that a reasonably well designed qualitative interview could give us better information than can an "objective" scale. In fact, there is even a quantitative approach, called cluster analysis, that I believe does a better job of identifying the types; when I use that approach, the Pittsburgh data look a little more as expected. Only 29 percent of the male violence in the court sample is identified as situational couple violence (compared to 37 percent with the arbitrary cutoff); 19 percent is identified as situational couple violence in the shelter sample (compared to 28 percent with the arbitrary cutoff). Michael P. Johnson, "Conflict and Control: Symmetry and Asymmetry in Domestic Violence," in *Couples in Conflict*, ed. Alan Booth, Ann C. Crouter, and Mari Clements (Mahwah, N.J.: Lawrence Erlbaum, 2001), 102. For a discussion of these different methodological approaches, see appendix A.

40. Looking, for example, at the frequency of violence from male partners involved in situational couple violence, we see that the average number of violent incidents is one in the general Pittsburgh sample, fifteen in the court sample, and twelve in the shelter sample. Similarly, situational couple violence involves serious injury to the woman in 19 percent of the cases in the general sample, 64 percent in the court sample, and 50 percent in the shelter sample.

41. If I use the cluster analysis approach, intimate terrorism is 97 percent male perpetrated. Situational couple violence is 56 percent male perpetrated. Johnson, "Conflict and Control," 100.

42. Nevertheless, the debate about gender symmetry continues, and there is very little published empirical work that addresses the issue in terms of the gender symmetry of intimate terrorism versus situational couple violence. There is one study (done in England) that quite closely replicates my findings. Graham-Kevan and Archer (2003) used control measures completely different from those I constructed from the Pittsburgh data and a sample that included 43 women shelter clients, 4 male batterer intervention participants, 104 students (mixed gender), and 97 male prisoners (not selected for domestic violence). They found that 87 percent of the intimate terrorists were men and 90 percent of the violent resisters were women, while situational couple violence was 45 percent male and 55 percent female. Their data also confirm the sampling pattern, with 75 percent of the men's violence in their nonselected sample being situational couple violence, as compared with 10 percent in their shelter sample. Nicola Graham-Kevan and John Archer, "Intimate Terrorism and Common Couple Violence: A Test of Johnson's Predictions in Four British Samples," *Journal of Interpersonal Violence* 18, no. 11 (2003): 1256, 1260.

There are also two recent studies that raise some questions about the gender distribution of intimate terrorism, finding intimate terrorism to be roughly gender symmetric. Nicola Graham-Kevan and John Archer, "Using Johnson's Domestic Violence Typology to Classify Men and Women in a Non-Selected Sample," unpublished (2005); Denis Laroche, "Aspects of the Context and Consequences of Domestic Violence: Situational Couple Violence and Intimate Terrorism in Canada," report, Government of Québec, Institut de la statistique du Québec, 2005. However, both of these studies use general samples. The problem with a general sample is that, as Graham-Kevan and Archer, and I, have shown, such samples include very little intimate terrorism. Because we have no well-defined criterion for the level of control required to identify intimate terrorism, authors generally resort to a cluster analysis approach. In a sample with little or no intimate terrorism, the cluster analysis will still identify a high-control cluster, but it is likely to consist mostly of situational couple violence, perhaps with a few cases of intimate terrorism. Thus, the gender distribution for the so-called intimate terrorism will be more like that of situational couple violence.

43. And mutual violent control, which is very rare.

44. Steinmetz, "The Battered Husband Syndrome."

45. I must admit, I used the mode here in part for dramatic effect, although it is

true that 11 percent of the intimate terrorists are reported to have been violent one hundred times, and 32 percent of the men involved in situational common violence had been violent only once. The modal figure of one hundred reported by wives for intimate terrorists is certainly inflated, because it is up in the range where women would not be giving precise estimates, but choosing numbers that approximated their experiences. The means and medians may not provide as dramatic a picture, but the differences are still clear. The means for intimate terrorism and situational couple violence are forty-four and ten, respectively. The medians are nineteen and three, respectively.

46. Remember that the types are defined in terms of control context, not the frequency or severity of the violence. The hypothesized differences in frequency and severity of the violence are derived from theory. It is assumed that attempts by husbands to exert general control over their wives will be met by considerable resistance in the United States, where marriage is seen by most women as a partnership. Thus, the intimate terrorist will in some cases turn to violence repeatedly and may escalate its severity in order to gain control.

Chapter 2. Intimate Terrorism: Controlling Your Partner (pages 25–47)

1. Feminist research has also provided considerable insight into the means by which women cope with intimate terrorism. Thus, there is also a growing body of feminist research on violent resistance, which will be addressed in the next chapter. Suzanne C. Swan and David L. Snow, "A Typology of Women's Use of Violence in Intimate Relationships," *Violence against Women* 8, no. 3 (2002).

2. It is also part of the definition of "intimate terrorism" that the victim is *not* violent and controlling. "Mutual violent control" (MVC) in which two violent and controlling partners fight for control of each other, almost certainly has quite a different dynamic than does intimate terrorism. Mutual violent control occurs, however, in such small numbers that there is as yet not a single study that includes enough cases for useful analysis. For example, the Pittsburgh data include only eight such couples. I had hopes that by the time I finished this book I might be able to include a chapter on MVC, but that will have to await the relevant research.

3. Catherine Kirkwood, *Leaving Abusive Partners: From the Scars of Survival to the Wisdom for Change* (Newbury Park, Calif.: Sage, 1993), 50.

4. This description of the basic features of intimate terrorism is organized around Mary Ann Dutton and Lisa Goodman's emerging theory of coercive control. Dutton and Goodman, "Coercion in Intimate Partner Violence: Toward a New Conceptualization," *Sex Roles* 52, no. 11/12 (2005). It is supported empirically by a vast number of studies of the experiences of women who come into contact with the major agencies that serve victims of domestic violence or that work with batterers. The best of these studies present a complex picture of the nature of intimate terrorism. Jacquelyn C. Campbell, ed., *Empowering Survivors of Abuse: Health Care for Battered Women and Their*

Children (Thousand Oaks, Calif.: Sage, 1998); Jacquelyn C. Campbell et al., "Voices of Strength and Resistance: A Contextual and Longitudinal Analysis of Women's Responses to Battering," *Journal of Interpersonal Violence* 13, no. 6 (1998); R. Emerson Dobash and Russell P. Dobash, *Violence against Wives: A Case against Patriarchy* (New York: Free Press, 1979); Donald G. Dutton, *The Batterer: A Psychological Profile*, trans. Susan K. Golant (New York: Basic Books, 1995); Edward W. Gondolf and Ellen R. Fisher, *Battered Women as Survivors: An Alternative to Treating Learned Helplessness* (Lexington, Mass.: D.C. Heath, 1988); Amy Holtzworth-Munroe, "A Typology of Men Who Are Violent toward Their Female Partners: Making Sense of the Heterogeneity in Husband Violence," *Current Directions in Psychological Science* 9, no. 4 (2000); Neil S. Jacobson and John M. Gottman, *When Men Batter Women: New Insights into Ending Abusive Relationships* (New York: Simon & Schuster, 1998); Ann Jones, *Women Who Kill* (Boston: Beacon Press, 1996); Kirkwood, *Leaving Abusive Partners*; Beth Richie, *Compelled to Crime: The Gender Entrapment of Battered Black Women* (New York: Routledge, 1996); Jan E. Stets, *Domestic Violence and Control* (New York: Springer-Verlag, 1988). For a general review of the domestic violence literature of the 1990s, see Johnson and Ferraro's decade review in the *Journal of Marriage and the Family*. Michael P. Johnson and Kathleen J. Ferraro, "Research on Domestic Violence in the 1990s: Making Distinctions," *Journal of Marriage and the Family* 62, no. 4 (2000).

5. Whenever I present a figure like this from the Pittsburgh data or the NVAWS regarding intimate terrorism, I have also checked the comparable number for men's situational couple violence and found it to be significantly different from intimate terrorism.

6. Quoted in Dobash and Dobash, *Violence against Wives*, 129.

7. Quoted in Ibid., 125.

8. Quoted in Kirkwood, *Leaving Abusive Partners*, 47.

9. Quoted in Ibid.

10. Quoted in Dobash and Dobash, *Violence against Wives*, 137.

11. Quoted in Valerie Nash Chang, *I Just Lost Myself: Psychological Abuse of Women in Marriage* (Westport, Conn.: Praeger, 1996), 74.

12. Quoted in Ibid., 110.

13. Quoted in Kirkwood, *Leaving Abusive Partners*, 56.

14. Quoted in Ibid., 57.

15. $F = 5.06$, $p < .007$. In addition, the variance for the intimate terrorist group was significantly smaller than that for the other two groups (Levene $F = 6.01$, $p < .003$). The median allowance for those living with intimate terrorism was $10.

16. Quoted in Kirkwood, *Leaving Abusive Partners*, 54.

17. In this section and elsewhere, I do not generally present the results of multiple studies by other authors in support of conclusions regarding the differences between intimate terrorism and situational couple violence. That is in part because there is still very little research published that actually operationalizes these distinctions, and in part to keep things simple in the main body of the book. There are, however, three re-

cent studies that do support the conclusions presented in this chapter. Graham-Kevan and Archer did two major studies in England confirming that intimate terrorism involves more frequent, escalating, and severe violence that produces more injuries than does situational couple violence. One of these uses a mixed sample drawn both from agencies and from a general population; the other uses only a general sample of students and staff at a university in England. Nicola Graham-Kevan and John Archer, "Intimate Terrorism and Common Couple Violence: A Test of Johnson's Predictions in Four British Samples," *Journal of Interpersonal Violence* 18, no. 11 (2003); Graham-Kevan and Archer, "Using Johnson's Domestic Violence Typology to Classify Men and Women in a Non-Selected Sample," unpublished. LaRoche, using a large general Canadian sample, also confirms the differences in the nature of the violence in intimate terrorism and situational couple violence. Denis Laroche, "Aspects of the Context and Consequences of Domestic Violence: Situational Couple Violence and Intimate Terrorism in Canada," report, Government of Québec, Institute de la statistique du Québec. LaRoche also confirms that victims of intimate terrorism (especially women) are more likely to need medical care, call the police, consult a counselor or psychologist, have their everyday activities disrupted, and fear for their lives (p. 17).

18. This is the percent of all intimate terrorists who (a) were violent more than once, and (b) for whom the violence escalated in severity. The figure for situational couple violence is 29 percent.

19. The figure for situational couple violence is 29 percent, a reminder that although situational couple violence is less likely to be severe, it *can* be deadly. See chapter 4 for a discussion of the violence in situational couple violence.

20. The few studies that claim to find considerable numbers of female intimate terrorists are based on general samples, thus raising questions about whether the intimate terrorism identified in them is actually intimate terrorism or merely situational couple violence combined with control levels that are high *for a general sample*. However, if we take these studies to provide some evidence for differences between female and male intimate terrorism, they show the levels of violence and negative consequences of intimate terrorism to be considerably lower for female intimate terrorists than for males. For example, LaRoche finds for what he calls "severe intimate terrorism" that 31 percent of female victims had reported more than ten events, compared with 17 percent of the male victims. Comparisons for negative outcomes are as follows: suffered injuries, 41 percent versus 15 percent; received medical attention, 18 percent versus 4 percent; consulted a counselor or psychologist, 29 percent versus 12 percent; had everyday activities disrupted, 32 percent versus 12 percent; and feared for his/her life, 39 percent versus 10 percent. LaRoche, "Aspects of the Context and Consequences of Domestic Violence."

21. Amy Holtzworth-Munroe and Gregory L. Stuart, "Typologies of Male Batterers: Three Subtypes and the Differences among Them," *Psychological Bulletin* 116, no. 3 (1994). I say "so-called batterers" because one of the three types (family-only) is clearly involved in situational couple violence rather than intimate terrorism.

22. Holtzworth-Munroe, "A Typology of Men"; Amy Holtzworth-Munroe et al., "Testing the Holtzworth-Munroe and Stuart (1994) Batterer Typology," *Journal of Consulting and Clinical Psychology* 68, no. 6 (2000); Amy Holtzworth-Munroe et al., "A Typology of Male Batterers: An Initial Examination," in *Violence in Intimate Relationships*, ed. Ximena B. Arriaga and Stuart Oskamp (Thousand Oaks, Calif.: Sage, 1999).

23. None of the research that I review in this section actually used measures of coercive control to develop its types, although in some of Holtzworth-Munroe's papers she demonstrates (after cluster identification) that only two of the three batterer types score high on a control measure. For this reason, and because I find Holtzworth-Munroe and her colleagues' labels to be somewhat confusing for people who are not familiar with the terminology of clinical psychology, I will use my own terms here rather than Holtzworth-Munroe's. I will label the family-only group, which does not score high on control, as actors in "situational couple violence"; the two high-control groups as "intimate terrorists"; the dysphoric/borderline group as "dependent intimate terrorists"; and the generally-violent/antisocial group as "antisocial intimate terrorists."

24. Holtzworth-Munroe uses Tolman's Psychological Maltreatment of Women Scale for this comparison. It includes items that tap two dimensions of control: dominance-isolation and emotional-verbal abuse. Richard M. Tolman, "The Development of a Measure of Psychological Maltreatment of Women by Their Male Partners," *Violence and Victims* 4, no. 3 (1989).

25. Richard B. Felson, *Violence and Gender Reexamined* (Washington, D.C.: American Psychological Association, 2002), 106.

26. The average effect size was .54 (p < .001). Sugarman and Frankel dismiss this general finding because the effects are heterogeneous across studies, but the two sources of that heterogeneity actually support the main finding of strong effects. First, the effects are very strong when there is a comparison group of nonviolent men (d = .72), but not when the comparison group is the norm group for the scale (d = .44). Of course, in the latter case, because the "norm" group certainly includes some violent men, the observed effect would be an underestimate of the true effect. Second, the other source of heterogeneity of effects strongly supports the feminist position that intimate terrorism is related to patriarchal attitudes (see n. 27 for this chapter and related text). David B. Sugarman and Susan L. Frankel, "Patriarchal Ideology and Wife-Assault: A Meta-Analytic Review," *Journal of Family Violence* 11, no. 1 (1996): 23.

27. d = .80 vs. d = −.14. Actually, what they found was that there are very strong effects in studies in which the men's attitudes are reported by their victims, and only weak effects when men report their own attitudes. What they do not note is that, in general, the studies that rely on victims' reports are agency studies, which, as I demonstrated in chapter 1 have a high concentration of intimate terrorism. Studies using men's reports are mostly general surveys that are dominated by situational couple violence. Thus, Sugarman and Frankel's overall conclusions should have been much stronger than they were. See Ibid., 23.

28. A number of other researchers using similar clustering techniques support the findings of the Holtzworth-Munroe group. Dutton, *The Batterer*; Edward W. Gondolf, "Who Are Those Guys? Toward a Behavioral Typology of Batterers," *Violence and Victims* 3, (Fall 1988); Daniel G. Saunders, "Feminist-Cognitive-Behavioral and Process-Psychodynamic Treatments for Men Who Batter: Interactions of Abuser Traits and Treatment Model," *Violence and Victims* 4, no. 4 (1996); Daniel G. Saunders, "A Typology of Men Who Batter: Three Types Derived from Cluster Analysis," *American Orthopsychiatry* 62, no. 2 (1992); Roger G. Tweed and Donald G. Dutton, "A Comparison of Impulsive and Instrumental Subgroups of Batterers," *Violence & Victims* 13, no. 3 (1998).

29. Because Jacobson and Gottman point out that practically all of the men they studied were psychologically abusive in addition to being violent, we can assume that their sample consisted almost entirely of intimate terrorists. Jacobson and Gottman, *When Men Batter Women*.

30. Ibid.; Neil S. Jacobson et al., "Affect, Verbal Content, and Psychophysiology in the Arguments of Couples with a Violent Husband," *Journal of Consulting and Clinical Psychology* 62, no. 5 (1994).

31. Jacobson and Gottman did not allow physical attacks during these arguments.

32. This research on risk markers for domestic violence should not be confused with the literature on risk markers for lethality. Campbell and her colleagues have done a series of studies comparing living victims of domestic violence with victims who have been killed by their partners, thus establishing risk markers for homicide *among victims of domestic violence*. In other words, women whose partners are violent and whose situations include these markers are at higher risk of homicide than are victims whose situations do not include these markers. Many of the markers they identify appear to be indications of intimate terrorism as opposed to situational couple violence. Let me warn again, however, that although the risk of lethality is higher for intimate terrorism than it is for situational couple violence, situational couple violence can be lethal, and safety planning should therefore be a high priority for work with either type of victim. Jacquelyn C. Campbell, "Prediction of Homicide of and by Battered Women," in *Assessing Dangerousness: Violence by Sexual Offenders, Batterers, and Child Abusers*, ed. Jacquelyn C. Campbell (Thousand Oaks, Calif.: Sage, 1995).

33. Glenda Kaufman Kantor and Jana L. Jasinski, "Dynamics and Risk Factors in Partner Violence," in *Partner Violence: A Comprehensive Review of 20 Years of Research*, ed. Jana L. Jasinski and Linda M. Williams (Thousand Oaks, Calif.: Sage, 1998), 16.

34. Johnson and Ferraro, "Making Distinctions," 957–58; Sandra M. Stith et al., "The Intergenerational Transmission of Spouse Abuse: A Meta-Analysis," *Journal of Marriage and the Family* 62, no. 3 (2000).

35. Murray A. Straus, Richard J. Gelles, and Suzanne K. Steinmetz, *Behind Closed Doors: Violence in the American Family* (Garden City, N.Y.: Doubleday, 1980). The authors define "wife beating" as the use of serious violence at least once in the previous twelve months (kicking, biting, or punching; hitting with an object; beating up; threatening with a knife or gun; using a knife or gun). On p. 100 they give figures for any kind of

violence in the previous twelve months; these figures indicate that 65 percent of men "who had seen parents physically attack each other" had not been violent, compared with 89 percent of those who had not seen their parents be violent toward each other. Again, we see an effect of parental violence, but an effect that is far from certain.

36. Odds Ratio = 21.67, Nagelkerke R-square = .44. The comparable figures for situational couple violence were Odds Ratio = 2.57 and R-square = .04.

37. Stith et al., "The Intergenerational Transmission of Spouse Abuse," 645.

38. d = .35 versus .11.

39. Jan E. Stets and Murray A. Straus, "The Marriage License as a Hitting License: A Comparison of Assaults in Dating, Cohabiting, and Married Couples," *Journal of Family Violence* 4, no. 2 (1989).

40. They use the range of violence used, rather than control, to distinguish among types of violence, but they do identify their "interpersonal conflict" group with situational couple violence and their "systematic abuse" group with intimate terrorism. Evidence for the validity of this analogy is that in their own data a measure of coercive control is much more closely associated with systematic abuse than it is with interpersonal conflict (p. 955). Ross Macmillan and Rosemary Gartner, "When She Brings Home the Bacon: Labor-Force Participation and the Risk of Spousal Violence against Women," *Journal of Marriage and the Family* 61, no. 4 (1999).

41. Odds Ratio = .54.

42. The Pittsburgh data cannot be used to investigate hypotheses about any variables likely to be associated with where people live, because the general sample consisted of women living on the same block as the women contacted through agencies, who therefore would be likely to be of the same race, socioeconomic status, and so on.

43. The zero-order Odds Ratio = .69. Controlling for race and income, the Odds Ratio = .63, p < .001.

44. Kantor and Jasinski, "Dynamics and Risk Factors in Partner Violence," 27.

45. Odds Ratio = .94, p = .22.

46. Johnson and Ferraro, "Making Distinctions," 953–54.

47. I am looking only at African Americans and whites here because the numbers in other categories are too small to allow a useful analysis in this restricted sample of married women. Tjaden and Thoennes have published data from the NVAWS that suggest that there are some other racial differences in risk of any partner violence (no distinctions). Patricia Tjaden and Nancy Thoennes, *Extent, Nature, and Consequences of Intimate Partner Violence: Findings from the National Violence Against Women Survey*, research report (Washington, D.C.: National Institute of Justice/Centers for Disease Control and Prevention, 1999).

48. Odds Ratio = .98; p = .97. There is, however, a marginally significant relationship with situational couple violence, which is eliminated by controls for education and income. See chapter 4.

49. The Odds Ratio after controlling for income and education is 1.58 (p = .21). In

contrast, there is no effect at all for situational couple violence. Even the zero-order Odds Ratio is only 1.08 (p = .82). See chapter 4.

50. Gerald T. Hotaling and David B. Sugarman, "An Analysis of Risk Markers in Husband to Wife Violence: The Current State of Knowledge," *Violence & Victims* 1, no. 2 (1986).

51. Odds Ratio = 1.13; p = .25. For situational couple violence, the Odds Ratio is 1.06 (p = .53).

52. Actually, there is a zero-order effect, which disappears when controls for education and income are introduced.

53. Campbell et al., "Voices of Strength and Resistance"; Kirkwood, *Leaving Abusive Partners*; Kathleen J. Ferraro, "Battered Women: Strategies for Survival," in *Violence among Intimate Partners: Patterns, Causes and Effects*, ed. Albert P. Carderelli (New York: Macmillan, 1997); Kathleen J. Ferraro, "The Dance of Dependency: A Genealogy of Domestic Violence Discourse," *Hypatia* 11, no. 4 (1996).

54. Kirkwood, *Leaving Abusive Partners*.

55. Stephanie Riger, Courtney Ahrens, and Amy Blickenstaff, "Measuring Interference with Employment and Education Reported by Women with Abusive Partners: Preliminary Data," in *Psychological Abuse in Violent Domestic Relations*, ed. K. Daniel O'Leary and Roland D. Maiuro (New York: Springer Publishing, 2001).

56 Susan Lloyd, "The Effects of Domestic Violence on Women's Employment," *Law & Policy* 19, no. 2 (1997); Susan Lloyd and Nina Taluc, "The Effects of Male Violence on Female Employment," *Violence Against Women* 5, no. 4 (1999).

57. Janel M. Leone et al., "Consequences of Male Partner Violence for Low-Income, Ethnic Women," *Journal of Marriage and Family* 66, no. 2 (2004). The data were from a study designed and carried out by Lloyd and her colleagues. Lloyd and Taluc, "The Effects of Male Violence on Female Employment."

58. Michael P. Johnson, "Conflict and Control: Gender Symmetry and Asymmetry in Domestic Violence," *Violence Against Women* 12, no. 11 (2006); Michael P. Johnson, Valerie Conklin, and Nividetha Menon, "The Effects of Different Types of Domestic Violence on Women: Intimate Terrorism Vs. Situational Couple Violence," paper presented at the National Council on Family Relations annual meeting (Houston, Texas, 2002); Michael P. Johnson and Janel M. Leone, "The Differential Effects of Patriarchal Terrorism and Common Couple Violence: Findings from the National Violence Against Women Survey," paper presented at the Tenth International Conference on Personal Relationships (Brisbane, Australia, 2000); Leone et al., "Consequences of Male Partner Violence." I will be citing data from the Johnson and Leone conference presentation, rather than the published version of that paper. The published paper involves fancier but less intuitive statistical approaches to the data. The findings were, of course, the same. Michael P. Johnson and Janel M. Leone, "The Differential Effects of Intimate Terrorism and Situational Couple Violence: Findings from the National Violence Against Women Survey," *Journal of Family Issues* 26, no. 3 (2005).

59. Johnson and Leone, "The Differential Effects of Patriarchal Terrorism and Common Couple Violence."

60. Leone et al., "Consequences of Male Partner Violence."

61. Jacquelyn C. Campbell and Karen L. Soeken, "Forced Sex and Intimate Partner Violence: Effects on Women's Risk and Women's Health," *Violence Against Women* 5, no. 9 (1999).

62. Jacquelyn C. Campbell et al., "Reproductive Health Consequences of Intimate Partner Violence: A Nursing Research Review," *Clinical Nursing Research* 9, no. 3 (2000).

63. Jacquelyn C. Campbell, "Making the Health Care System an Empowerment Zone for Battered Women: Health Consequences, Policy Recommendations, Introduction, and Overview," in *Empowering Survivors of Abuse*, 5–6.

64. Janel M. Leone et al., "Consequences of Different Types of Domestic Violence for Low-Income, Ethnic Women: A Control-Based Typology of Male-Partner Violence," paper presented at the International Network on Personal Relationships (Prescott, Arizona, June 2001), 20.

65. Cheryl Ann Sutherland, "Investigating the Effects of Intimate Partner Violence on Women's Health (Physical Abuse, Suicide Ideation, Depression)," PhD diss., Michigan State University, 1999.

66. Cheryl A. Sutherland, Deborah I. Bybee, and Cris M. Sullivan, "Beyond Bruises and Broken Bones: The Joint Effects of Stress and Injuries on Battered Women's Health," *American Journal of Community Psychology* 30, no. 5 (2002).

67. Quoted in Kirkwood, *Leaving Abusive Partners*, 44.

68. Ibid., 114–33.

69. Rudy J. Aguilar and Narina Nunez Nightingale, "The Impact of Specific Battering Experience on the Self-Esteem of Abused Women," *Journal of Family Violence* 9, no. 1 (1994); Michele Cascardi and K. Daniel O'Leary, "Depressive Symptomology, Self-Esteem, and Self-Blame in Battered Women," *Journal of Family Violence* 7, no. 4 (1992); Chang, *I Just Lost Myself*; Kirkwood, *Leaving Abusive Partners*; Tammy A. Orava, Peter J. McLeod, and Donald Sharpe, "Perceptions of Control, Depressive Symptomatology, and Self-Esteem of Women in Transition from Abusive Relationships," *Journal of Family Violence* 11, no. 2 (1996); Nancy Felipe Russo et al., "Intimate Violence and Black Women's Health," *Women's Health* 3, no. 3–4 (1997); Leslie A. Sackett and Daniel G. Saunders, "The Impact of Different Forms of Psychological Abuse on Battered Women," *Violence and Victims* 14, no. 1 (1999).

70. Kirkwood, *Leaving Abusive Partners*, 68.

71. Quoted in Chang, *I Just Lost Myself*, 110.

72. Quoted in Dobash and Dobash, *Violence against Wives*, 138.

73. The figures are 36 percent and 14 percent for those experiencing situational couple violence. $X^2 = 11.26$, df = 3, p < .01.

74. The figures are 26 percent and 9 percent for situational couple violence. $X^2 = 20.64$, df = 4, p < .001.

75. Sackett and Saunders, "The Impact of Different Forms of Psychological Abuse";

Daniel G. Saunders, "Posttraumatic Stress Symptom Profiles of Battered Women: A Comparison of Survivors in Two Settings," *Violence and Victims* 9, no. 1 (1994); Cheryl Sutherland, Deborah Bybee, and Cris Sullivan, "The Long-Term Effects of Battering on Women's Health," *Women's Health: Research on Gender, Behavior, and Policy* 4, no. 1 (1998).

76 Alfred DeMaris and Steven Swinford, "Female Victims of Spousal Violence: Factors Influencing Their Level of Fearfulness," *Family Relations* 45 (1996); Elaine Grandin, Eugen Lupri, and Merlin B. Brinkerhoff, "Couple Violence and Psychological Distress," *Canadian Journal of Public Health* 89, no. 1 (1998); Lynn Magdol et al., "Gender Differences in Partner Violence in a Birth Cohort of 21-Year-Olds: Bridging the Gap between Clinical and Epidemiological Approaches," *Journal of Consulting & Clinical Psychology* 65, no. 1 (1997).

77. DeMaris and Swinford, "Female Victims of Spousal Violence."

78. Jacqueline M. Golding, "Intimate Partner Violence as a Risk Factor for Mental Disorders: A Meta-Analysis," *Journal of Family Violence* 14, no. 2 (1999). Some of these studies also assessed rates of depression in a comparison group and found that the odds of being depressed were nearly four times higher for battered women than for the comparison groups.

79. Golding, "Intimate Partner Violence as a Risk Factor for Mental Disorders."

80. Johnson and Leone, "The Differential Effects of Patriarchal Terrorism and Common Couple Violence."

81. Saunders, "Posttraumatic Stress Symptom Profiles."

82. Johnson and Leone, "The Differential Effects of Patriarchal Terrorism and Common Couple Violence." For another approach to the same data, see Johnson and Leone, "The Differential Effects of Intimate Terrorism and Situational Couple Violence."

83. Kirkwood, *Leaving Abusive Partners*, 81–86.

84. Sutherland, Bybee, and Sullivan, "The Long-Term Effects of Battering."

85. Cris M. Sullivan and Deborah I. Bybee, "Reducing Violence Using Community-Based Advocacy for Women with Abusive Partners," *Journal of Consulting & Clinical Psychology* 67, no. 1 (1999).

86. Janel M. Leone, Michael P. Johnson, and Catherine L. Cohan, "Help-Seeking among Women in Violent Relationships: Factors Associated with Formal and Informal Help Utilization," paper presented at the National Council on Family Relations annual meeting (Vancouver, British Columbia, November 2003).

87. Maria Testa and Kenneth E. Leonard, "The Impact of Marital Aggression on Women's Psychological and Marital Functioning in a Newlywed Sample," *Journal of Family Violence* 16, no. 2 (2001).

88. The response options for this question are somewhat problematic, involving what appears to be quite a leap between options 4 and 5: 1 = Never; 2 = Once; 3 = 2 or 3 times; 4 = Several times; 5 = Often. These numbers are for response options 4 and 5. $X^2 = 50.17$; $df = 8$; $p < .001$.

89. $X^2 = 24.79$; $df = 8$; $p < .002$.

90. These are 1 and 2 on a ten-point scale that is anchored at one end at "Not at all happy." The following numbers are 9 or 10 at the other end of the scale, anchored at "Very happy." X2 = 125.42; df = 18; p < .001.

91. X^2 = 156.93; df = 8; p < .001.

92. X^2 = 117.81; df = 8; p < .001.

93. Kirkwood, *Leaving Abusive Partners*.

94. Evan Stark, *Coercive Control: The Entrapment of Women in Personal Life* (New York: Oxford University Press, 2007).

95. Ibid., 380–88.

96. Ibid., 5.

97. I think it might be useful to address the terminological issue more fully at this point. Stark does not like my use of the term "intimate terrorism" for two reasons (Stark, pp. 103–6). First, he argues that coercive control is often involved after a couple no longer lives together or in relationships that do not involve living together, and thus he does not like the word "intimate." From my point of view, what the term "intimate" does is to make it clear that we are not talking about strangers, but about a couple who now has or has had in the past some sort of ongoing romantic involvement. Second, he does not like the term "terrorism" because it has "little to do with the tactics used by terrorists" (p. 105). I chose the term "terrorism" because the victims are in fact terrorized by their partners, living in fear in their everyday lives. However, in the ten to fifteen years since I began to use that term, politically-inspired terrorism has become such a part of everyday life in the United States that the term does create some unfortunate associations. Attorneys working in family court have told me that they would never use such a term in court because it is too inflammatory. Although, to avoid confusion, I am not inclined to change my own terminology once again, in situations in which the intimate context is obvious and can be taken for granted (such as in a child custody hearing or a domestic violence trial), I think it might be useful for many purposes to refer to intimate terrorism as "violent coercive control."

Chapter 3. Fighting Back: Violent Resistance (pages 48–59)

1. James H. Kleckner, "Wife Beaters and Beaten Wives: Co-Conspirators in Crimes of Violence," *Psychology: A Journal of Human Behavior* 15, no. 1 (1978); Natalie Shainess, "Vulnerability to Violence: Masochism as Process," *American Journal of Psychotherapy* 33, no. 2 (1979); John E. Snell, Richard J. Rosenwald, and Ames Robey, "The Wife-beater's Wife," *Archives of General Psychiatry* 11, no. 2 (1964).

2. Lenore E. Walker, *The Battered Woman Syndrome* (New York: Springer, 1984).

3. Edward W. Gondolf and Ellen R. Fisher, *Battered Women as Survivors: An Alternative to Treating Learned Helplessness* (Lexington, Mass.: D. C. Health, 1988), 30.

4. Kathleen J. Ferraro, "Battered Women: Strategies for Survival," in *Violence among Intimate Partners: Patterns, Causes, and Effects*, ed. Albert P. Carderelli (New York: Macmillan, 1997).

5. Jessica G. Burke et al., "The Process of Ending Abuse in Intimate Relationships:

A Qualitative Exploration of the Transtheoretical Model," *Violence Against Women* 7, no. 10 (2001).

6. Walker, *The Battered Woman Syndrome.*

7. Ferraro, "Battered Women," 126.

8. Quoted in Ibid., 129.

9. Quoted in Ibid., 128–29.

10. Valerie Nash Chang, *I Just Lost Myself: Psychological Abuse of Women in Marriage* (Westport, Conn.: Praeger, 1996).

11. Janel M. Leone, "Help-Seeking among Women in Violent Relationships: Testing a Control-Based Typology of Partner Violence," PhD diss., Department of Individual and Family Studies, Pennsylvania State University, 2003, 56; Janel M. Leone, Michael P. Johnson, and Catherine L. Cohan, "Help-Seeking among Women in Violent Relationships: Factors Associated with Formal and Informal Help Utilization," paper presented at the National Council on Family Relations annual meeting (Vancouver, British Columbia, November 2003). This study also shows that although women experiencing situational couple violence are just as likely as those experiencing intimate terrorism to talk it over with family or friends, they are not as likely to seek formal help. For the same data presented with fancier statistics, but less accessibly, see Janel M. Leone, Michael P. Johnson, and Catherine M. Cohan, "Victim Help-Seeking: Differences between Intimate Terrorism and Situational Couple Violence," *Family Relations* 56, no. 5 (2007).

12. Mildred Daley Pagelow, *Woman-Battering: Victims and Their Experiences* (Newbury Park, Calif.: Sage, 1981), 67.

13. Susan L. Miller, *Victims as Offenders: The Paradox of Women's Violence in Relationships* (New Brunswick, N.J.: Rutgers, 2005). Actually, one of the ninety-five was not court-mandated into the program.

14. Quoted in Ibid., 120–21. It should be noted that although all of these cases involve some violence on the part of the woman's partner, it is possible that some of them involve situational couple violence. Miller's approach is incident-focused enough that we cannot distinguish relationships in which arguments escalate into violence from those in which there is a clear pattern of intimate terrorism on the part of the male partner.

15. Quoted in Ibid., 122–23.

16. Quoted in Pagelow, *Woman-Battering*, 67.

17. Ronet Bachman and Dianne Cyr Carmody, "Fighting Fire with Fire: The Effects of Victim Resistance in Intimate Versus Stranger Perpetrated Assaults against Females," *Journal of Family Violence* 9, no. 4 (1994).

18. The final 5 percent of the violence in her sample is what she calls "generalized violent behavior" and appears from the stories to primarily be situational couple violence rather than violent resistance. These were women with chronic problems of violence toward their partners and others.

19. Quoted in Miller, *Victims as Offenders*, 119.

20. Campbell et al., "Voices of Strength and Resistance: A Contextual and Longitudinal Analysis of Women's Responses to Battering," *Journal of Interpersonal Violence* 13, no. 6 (1998).

21. Unfortunately, these are not idle threats. For a discussion of the stalking and increased violence that can follow a woman after she leaves, see appendix B.

22. Catherine Kirkwood, *Leaving Abusive Partners: From the Scars of Survival to the Wisdom for Change* (Newbury Park, Calif.: Sage, 1993).

23. Myra Marx Ferree, Judith Lorber, and Beth B. Hess, introduction, to *Revisioning Gender*, ed. Myra Marx Ferree, Judith Lorber, and Beth B. Hess (Walnut Creek, Calif.: AltaMira, 2000); Barbara Risman, "Gender as a Social Structure: Theory Wrestling with Activism," *Gender & Society* 18, no. 4 (2004).

24. R. Emerson Dobash and Russell P. Dobash, *Violence against Wives: A Case against Patriarchy* (New York: Free Press, 1979); Dobash and Dobash, *Women, Violence and Social Change* (New York: Routledge, 1992); Kersti Yllö and Michele Bograd, eds., *Feminist Perspectives on Wife Abuse* (Newbury Park, Calif.: Sage, 1988). See appendix C for more discussion of the gendering of intimate partner violence.

25. Eva Schlesinger Buzawa, *Domestic Violence: The Criminal Justice Response* (Thousand Oaks, Calif.: Sage, 2003).

26. Dobash and Dobash, *Women, Violence and Social Change*; Susan Schechter, *Women and Male Violence: The Visions and Struggles of the Battered Women's Movement* (Boston: South End Press, 1982); Evan Stark, *Coercive Control: The Entrapment of Women in Personal Life* (New York: Oxford University Press, 2007), 21–80. These changes are probably a major source of the recent dramatic decline in fatal intimate partner violence against men in the United States, as more women are able to escape from abusive relationships. Callie Marie Rennison, *Intimate Partner Violence, 1993–2001*, special report, U.S. Department of Justice, Bureau of Justice Statistics (2003).

27. Angela Browne, *When Battered Women Kill*, (New York: Free Press, 1987).

28. Ibid., 88–89.

29. Ibid., 119–20.

30. Angela Browne, Kirk R. Williams, and Donald G. Dutton, "Homicide between Intimate Partners: A 20-Year Review," in *Homicide: A Sourcebook of Social Research*, ed. M. Dwayne Smith and Margaret A. Zahn (Thousand Oaks, Calif.: Sage, 1999), 158.

31. Rennison, "Intimate Partner Violence"; U.S. Federal Bureau of Investigation, "Crime in the United States 2005," *Uniform Crime Reports* (2006). The number was 1,357 in 1976. For comparison, 1,600 men murdered their wives or girlfriends in 1976; in 2004, that figure was 1,159, a 28 percent decrease.

Chapter 4. Conflicts That Turn Violent:
Situational Couple Violence (pages 60–71)

1. Thomas Bradbury, Ronald Rogge, and Erika Lawrence, "Reconsidering the Role of Conflict in Marriage," in *Couples in Conflict*, ed. Alan Booth, Ann C. Crouter, and Mari Clements (Mahwah, N.J.: Lawrence Erlbaum Associates, 2001).

2. Richard J. Gelles and Murray A. Straus, *Intimate Violence: The Causes and Consequences of Abuse in the American Family* (New York: Simon & Schuster, 1988).

3. Ross Macmillan and Rosemary Gartner, "When She Brings Home the Bacon: Labor-Force Participation and the Risk of Spousal Violence against Women," *Journal of Marriage and the Family* 61, no. 4 (1999); Jan E. Stets and Murray A. Straus, "The Marriage License as a Hitting License: A Comparison of Assaults in Dating, Cohabiting, and Married Couples," *Journal of Family Violence* 4, no. 2 (1989); Murray A. Straus, "Prevalence of Violence against Dating Partners by Male and Female University Students Worldwide," *Violence Against Women* 10 (2004).

4. John Archer, "Sex Differences in Aggression between Heterosexual Partners: A Meta-Analytic Review," *Psychological Bulletin* 126, no. 5 (2000); Michael P. Johnson, "Domestic Violence: The Intersection of Gender and Control," in *Gender Violence: Interdisciplinary Perspectives*, 2nd ed., ed. Laura L. O'Toole, Jessica R. Schiffman, and Margie Kiter Edwards (New York: New York University Press, in press).

5. Michael S. Kimmel, "'Gender Symmetry' in Domestic Violence: A Substantive and Methodological Research Review," *Violence Against Women* 8, no. 11 (2002); Barbara J. Morse, "Beyond the Conflict Tactics Scale: Assessing Gender Differences in Partner Violence," *Violence and Victims* 10, no. 4 (1995); Daniel G. Saunders, "Are Physical Assaults by Wives and Girlfriends a Major Social Problem? A Review of the Literature," *Violence against Women* 8, no. 12 (2002); Jan E. Stets and Murray A. Straus, "Gender Differences in Reporting Marital Violence and Its Medical and Psychological Consequences," in *Physical Violence in American Families: Risk Factors and Adaptation to Violence in 8,145 Families*, ed. Murray A. Straus and Richard J. Gelles (New Brunswick, N.J.: Transaction Press, 1990).

6. Michael P. Johnson, Valerie Conklin, and Niveditha Menon, "The Effects of Different Types of Domestic Violence on Women: Intimate Terrorism Vs. Situational Couple Violence."

7. Richard J. Gelles, *The Violent Home* (Newbury Park, CA: Sage, 1987 [1974]), 49.

8. Straus and Gelles, eds., *Physical Violence in American Families*.

9. For male intimate terrorists, about one in five in the Pittsburgh data are involved in chronic violence.

10. The figure for intimate terrorism was 67 percent.

11. I expect that the factors that produce single-incident (or rare-incident) situational couple violence are relatively idiosyncratic and not amenable to such causal analysis.

12. Richard J. Gelles and Murray A. Straus, "Determinants of Violence in the Family: Toward a Theoretical Integration," in *Contemporary Theories About the Family*, ed. Wesley Burr, et al. (New York: Free Press, 1979); Murray A. Straus, Richard J. Gelles, and Suzanne K. Steinmetz, *Behind Closed Doors: Violence in the American Family* (Garden City, N.J.: Doubleday, 1980).

13. Straus, Gelles, and Steinmetz, *Behind Closed Doors*, 163.

14. They use the range of violence used, rather than control, to distinguish among

types of violence, but they do identify their "interpersonal conflict" group with situational couple violence and their "systematic abuse" group with intimate terrorism. Evidence for the validity of this analogy is that in their own data a measure of coercive control is much more closely associated with systematic abuse than it is with interpersonal conflict (p. 955). Macmillan and Gartner, "When She Brings Home the Bacon."

15. Odds Ratio = .54.

16. Glenda Kaufman Kantor and Jana L. Jasinski, "Dynamics and Risk Factors in Partner Violence," in *Partner Violence: A Comprehensive Review of 20 Years of Research*, ed. Jana L. Jasinski and Linda M. Williams (Thousand Oaks, Calif.: Sage, 1998), 27. In my own analysis of the NVAWS data, the Odds Ratio for income and intimate terrorism was .94 (p =. 22).

17. The table from which these data are taken refers to the following violent acts: kicking, biting, hitting with a fist, hitting or trying to hit with something, beating up, and threatening with or using a knife or a gun.

18. Straus, Gelles, and Steinmetz, *Behind Closed Doors*, 129.

19. Hotaling and Sugarman, "An Analysis of Risk Markers in Husband to Wife Violence: The Current State of Knowledge," *Violence and Victims* 1, no. 2 (1986).

20. Straus, Gelles, and Steinmetz, *Behind Closed Doors*, 171.

21. Hotaling and Sugarman, "An Analysis of Risk Markers."

22. Kay Pasley, Jennifer Kerpelman, and Douglas E. Guilbert, "Gendered Conflict, Identity Disruption, and Marital Instability: Expanding Gottman's Model," *Journal of Social and Personal Relationships* 18, no. 1 (2001).

23. Straus, Gelles, and Steinmetz, *Behind Closed Doors*, 157. In order of frequency, the others were "affection and sex relations," "social activities and entertainment," "managing the money," and "things about the children."

24. Kantor and Jasinski, "Dynamics and Risk Factors," 20–23.

25. Glenda Kaufman Kantor and Murray A. Straus, "The 'Drunken Bum' Theory of Wife Beating," in *Physical Violence in American Families*.

26. Ibid., 210–11.

27. As Kantor and Straus point out, another important possibility is a correlated third factor. For example, men who drink heavily may be caught up in a version of male culture that endorses not only heavy drinking, but also male entitlement that will allow no "backtalk" from wives; this sense of male entitlement would play out in any arguments, not just those focused on the use of alcohol. Ibid.

28. Straus, Gelles, and Steinmetz, *Behind Closed Doors*, 161–63.

29. Dominic A. Infante and C. J. Wigley, "Verbal Aggressiveness: An Interpersonal Model and Measure," *Communication Monographs* 53, no. 1 (1986); Teresa Chandler Sabourin, "The Role of Communication in Verbal Abuse between Partners," in *Family Violence from a Communication Perspective*, ed. Dudley D. Cahn and Sally A. Lloyd (Thousand Oaks, Calif.: Sage, 1996); Murray A. Straus and C. Sweet, "Verbal/Symbolic Ag-

gression in Couples: Incidence Rates and Relationship to Personal Characteristics," *Journal of Marriage and the Family* 54, no. 2 (1992).

30. Michael E. Roloff, "The Catalyst Hypothesis: Conditions under Which Coercive Communication Leads to Physical Aggression," in *Family Violence from a Communication Perspective.*

31. Dominic A. Infante, Teresa A. Chandler, and Jill E. Rudd, "Test of an Argumentative Skill Deficiency Model of Interspousal Violence," *Communication Monographs* 56, no. 2 (1989): 166.

32. Clyde M. Feldman and Carl A. Ridley, "The Role of Conflict-Based Communication Responses and Outcomes in Male Domestic Violence toward Female Partners," *Journal of Social and Personal Relationships* 17, no. 4–5 (2000); Dominic A. Infante, Scott A. Myers, and Rick A. Buerkel, "Argument and Verbal Aggression in Constructive and Destructive Family and Organizational Disagreements," *Western Journal of Communication* 58, no. 2 (1994); Dominic A. Infante and Andrew S. Rancer, "Argumentativeness and Verbal Aggressiveness: A Review of Recent Theory and Research," in *Communication Yearbook 1996*, ed. Brant R. Burleson (Thousand Oaks, Calif.: Sage, 1996); Loreen N. Olson, "Exploring 'Common Couple Violence' in Heterosexual Romantic Relationships," *Western Journal of Communication* 66, no. 1 (2002); Carl A. Ridley and Clyde M. Feldman, "Female Domestic Violence toward Male Partners: Exploring Conflict Responses and Outcomes," *Journal of Family Violence* 18, no. 3 (2003); Teresa Chandler Sabourin, "The Role of Negative Reciprocity in Spouse Abuse: A Relational Control Analysis," *Journal of Applied Communication Research* 23, no. 4 (1995).

33. Olson, "Exploring 'Common Couple Violence,'" 118.

34. In dramatic contrast, Olson identifies another violent type of couple in which the communication pattern is a highly unusual male demand/female withdraw. Her description of these couples suggests that they are dealing with intimate terrorism, in which the wife is afraid to engage in a disagreement with her husband.

35. Remember that there are two basic types of intimate terrorists. Those whom I have called "antisocial" score high on antisociality, hostility toward women, and impulsiveness, but do not suffer from the personality disorders that characterize the "emotionally dependent" intimate terrorists (fear of abandonment, passive-aggressiveness, depression, anxiety, post-traumatic stress disorder, etc.).

36. Feldman and Ridley, "The Role of Conflict-Based Communication Responses and Outcomes"; Amy Holtzworth-Munroe et al., "Do Subtypes of Maritally Violent Men Continue to Differ over Time?" *Journal of Consulting and Clinical Psychology* 71, no. 4 (2003); Amy Holtzworth-Munroe et al., "Testing the Holtzworth-Munroe and Stuart (1994) Batterer Typology," *Journal of Consulting and Clinical Psychology* 68, no. 6 (2000).

37. Kantor and Jasinski, "Dynamics and Risk Factors," 16.

38. Michael P. Johnson and Kathleen J. Ferraro, "Research on Domestic Violence in the 1990s: Making Distinctions," *Journal of Marriage and the Family* 62, no. 4 (2000),

957–58; Sandra M. Stith et al., "The Intergenerational Transmission of Spouse Abuse: A Meta-Analysis," *Journal of Marriage and the Family* 62, no. 3 (2000).

39. Again, remember that the one study that investigated this issue with separate samples of intimate terrorism and situational couple violence found minimal effects for situational couple violence (Odds Ratio = 2.57 and Nagelkerke R-square = .04), but a strong effect for intimate terrorism (Odds Ratio = 21.67, R-square = .44). Michael P. Johnson and Alison Cares, "Effects and Non-Effects of Childhood Experiences of Family Violence on Adult Partner Violence," paper presented at the annual meeting, National Council on Family Relations (Orlando, Florida, 2004).

40. The zero-order Odds Ratio = .81, as compared to .69 for intimate terrorism.

41. Johnson and Ferraro, "Making Distinctions," 953–54.

42. The zero-order Odds Ratio is .57, p < .05. Controlling for income, the Odds Ratio is .67, p = .21. For a Latino vs. non-Latino comparison, there is no effect of ethnicity: Odds Ratio = 1.08, p = .82.

43. Michael P. Johnson, "Conflict and Control: Symmetry and Asymmetry in Domestic Violence," in *Couples in Conflict*, ed. Alan Booth, Ann C. Crouter, and Mari Clements (Mahwah, N.J.: Lawrence Erlbaum, 2001); Johnson, Conklin, and Menon, "The Effects of Different Types of Domestic Violence on Women."

44. Stets and Straus, "Gender Differences in Reporting Marital Violence," 157.

45. Michael P. Johnson and Janel M. Leone, "The Differential Effects of Intimate Terrorism and Situational Couple Violence: Findings from the National Violence Against Women Survey," *Journal of Family Issues* 26, no. 3 (2005).

46. Stets and Straus, "Gender Differences in Reporting Marital Violence," 158–161.

47. Johnson, Conklin, and Menon, "The Effects of Different Types of Domestic Violence on Women." The comparable figures for intimate terrorism were 50 percent and 74 percent, respectively.

Chapter 5. Implications for Intervention, Prevention, and Research (pages 71–86)

1. R. Emerson Dobash and Russell P. Dobash, *Women, Violence and Social Change* (New York: Routledge, 1992); Susan Schecter, *Women and Male Violence: The Visions and Struggles of the Battered Women's Movement* (Boston: South End Press, 1982); Evan Stark, *Coercive Control: The Entrapment of Women in Personal Life* (New York: Oxford University Press, 2007).

2. Many of these agencies also provide services for male victims of intimate partner violence in both same-sex and heterosexual relationships.

3. This is a bit of an oversimplification. There is considerable variability among shelters and continuing conflict within shelters regarding adherence to the feminist empowerment model that was the model for many of the early shelters. Stark, *Coercive Control*, 73–80.

4. Jacquelyn C. Campbell, ed., *Assessing Dangerousness: Violence by Sexual Offenders, Batterers, and Child Abusers* (Thousand Oaks, Calif.: Sage, 1995).

5. See Davies et al., for a more thorough discussion of safety planning. Jill Davies, Eleanor Lyon, and Diane Monti-Catania, *Safety Planning with Battered Women: Complex Lives/Difficult Choices* (Thousand Oaks, Calif.: Sage, 1998).

6. Christina DeJong and Amanda K. Burgess-Proctor, "A Summary of Personal Protection Order Statutes in the United States," *Violence Against Women* 12, no. 1 (2006).

7. Amanda K. Burgess-Proctor, "Evaluating the Efficacy of Protection Orders for Victims of Domestic Violence," *Women and Criminal Justice* 15 (2003); Eve Schlesinger Buzawa and Carl G. Buzawa, eds., *Do Arrests and Restraining Orders Work?* (Thousand Oaks, Calif.: Sage Publications, 1996); L. E. Ross, "Do Arrests and Restraining Orders Work?" *International Journal of Offender Therapy and Comparative Criminology* 42, no. 2 (1998). Law enforcement agencies, and specific officers, differ greatly in their handling of such orders of protection. As I am writing this, there is a case in my local newspaper of a murder-suicide in which the sheriff's department failed to enforce an order to confiscate an intimate terrorist's weapons. This is why the coordinated community response plans discussed below are so important.

8. Quite unlike the situation in most research, in which assessments are made on the basis of one interview or information from one questionnaire. See appendix A.

9. Eva Schlesinger Buzawa, *Domestic Violence: The Criminal Justice Response* (Thousand Oaks, Calif.: Sage, 2003).

10. Linda G. Mills, *Insult to Injury: Rethinking Our Responses to Intimate Abuse* (Princeton, N.J.: Princeton University Press, 2003). Linda Mills has attracted considerable attention with her critique of mandatory arrest and prosecution policies. Although her major point, that mandatory policies ignore the variability among cases of domestic violence, is in essential harmony with my analysis, her couching of her critique as an attack on "mainstream feminists" often undermines her credibility. For example, she claims that mandatory arrest policies are a function of mainstream feminists' adherence to Lenore Walker's learned helplessness theory, which, she argues, leads them to a view of battered women as weak, helpless victims for whom law enforcement (and the feminists) must make decisions because "victims" are incapable of acting in their own best interests. This argument ignores the fact that survivor theory has been the mainstream feminist analysis of battered women for at least twenty years. Feminists long ago debunked the idea that battered women were helpless victims. Since the 1980s, advocacy training has been rooted in feminist research that clearly established the active role that battered women play in either resisting their victimization within the relationship or taking the steps needed to allow themselves to escape the relationship safely. Jacquelyn C. Campbell, Linda Rose, Joan Kub, and Daphne Nedd, "Voices of Strength and Resistance: A Contextual and Longitudinal Analysis of Women's Responses to Battering," *Journal of Interpersonal Violence* 13, no. ' (1998); Kathleen J. Ferraro, "Battered Women: Strategies for Survival," in *Vio'* *among Intimate Partners: Patterns, Causes and Effects*, ed. Albert P. Carderelli (Ne' Macmillan, 1997); Edward W. Gondolf, Albert P. Carderelli, and Ellen R. F' *tered Women as Survivors: An Alternative to Treating Learned Helplessness* (Lexir'

D. C. Heath, 1988); Catherine Kirkwood, *Leaving Abusive Partners: From the Scars of Survival to the Wisdom for Change* (Newbury Park, Calif.: Sage, 1993). Marilyn Merritt-Gray and Judith Wuest, "Counteracting Abuse and Breaking Free: The Process of Leaving Revealed through Women's Voices," *Health Care for Women International* 16, no. 5 (1995).

Mills also argues, I believe correctly, that mandatory policies disempower battered women, substituting law enforcement decisions for the decisions of the victims regarding arrest and prosecution. However, once again she insists on writing as if feminists were totally unaware of this problem, when in fact mainstream feminist analyses of mandatory arrest policies have always addressed the tension between such mandatory policies and the feminist empowerment model that has long been the heart of the battered women's movement. From early in the battered women's movement, a tension has existed between the feminist empowerment model and the service-delivery model more typical of social work; and, indeed, there is considerable variability among shelters and among advocates within each shelter in the extent to which they practice what Davies and her coauthors call "woman-defined advocacy." This is "advocacy that builds a partnership between advocates and battered women, and ultimately has each battered woman defining the advocacy and help she needs." Davies, Lyon, and Monti-Catania, *Safety Planning with Battered Women*, 3. However, as these authors put it, this approach "builds on the historic commitment of the battered women's movement to empower battered women" (p. 7) that is ignored by Mills.

11. Susan L. Miller, *Victims as Offenders: The Paradox of Women's Violence in Relationships* (New Brunswick, N.J.: Rutgers, 2005).

12. Canada's National Judicial Institute sponsored a 2007 national conference for judges and prosecutors organized around distinctions among types of intimate partner violence.

13. Michael P. Johnson, Review of *Restorative Justice and Family Violence*, ed. by Heather Strang and John Braithwaite, *Contemporary Sociology: A Journal of Reviews* 33, no. 1 (2004); Heather Strang and John Braithwaite, eds., *Restorative Justice and Family Violence* (Cambridge: Cambridge University Press, 2002).

14. For further discussion, see Elizabeth P. Cramer, "Unintended Consequences of Constructing Criminal Justice as a Dominant Paradigm in Understanding and Intervening in Intimate Partner Violence," *Women's Studies Quarterly* 33 (2005); Hema Hargovan, "Restorative Justice and Domestic Violence: Some Exploratory Thoughts," *Agenda* 66 (2005); Lois Presser and Emily Gaarder, "Can Restorative Justice Reduce Battering? Some Preliminary Considerations," *Social Justice* 27, no. 1 (2000).

15. Michael P. Johnson, "Restorative Justice and Family Violence," *Contemporary Sociology: A Journal of Reviews* 33, no. 1 (2004): 97–98; Mills, *Insult to Injury*, 101–48.

16. Mills, *Insult to Injury*, 104.

17. Julia C. Babcock, Charles E. Green, and Chet Robie, "Does Batterers' Treatment Work? A Meta-Analytic Review of Domestic Violence Treatment," *Clinical Psychology Review* 23, no. 8 (2004).

18. Christopher I. Eckhardt et al., "Readiness to Change, Partner Violence Sub-

types, and Treatment Outcomes among Men in Treatment for Partner Assault," paper presented at the International Family Violence Conference (Portsmouth, New Hampshire, July 2003). The group with a 9 percent completion rate was composed of antisocial intimate terrorists; the group with 38 percent completion was made up of emotionally-dependent intimate terrorists.

19. Kahni Clements et al., "Testing the Holtzworth-Munroe et al. (2000) Batterer Typology among Court-Referred Maritally Violent Men," paper presented at the Association for the Advancement of Behavior Therapy annual meeting (Reno, Nevada, November 2002). The problem with this study is that it does not have a no-treatment control group. Thus, although the results may be suggestive regarding the effects of treatment, the results could be due entirely to differences among these groups in likelihood of continuing violence regardless of treatment. It is also important to keep in mind when interpreting the recidivism results that all of these men had been court-mandated to programs. Thus, their recidivism rates reflect the effects not only of treatment, but also of having been adjudicated by the criminal justice system.

20. Daniel G. Saunders, "Feminist-Cognitive-Behavioral and Process-Psychodynamic Treatments for Men Who Batter: Interactions of Abuser Traits and Treatment Model," Violence and Victims 4, no. 4 (1996).

21. Ellen Pence and Michael Paymar, Education Groups for Men Who Batter: The Duluth Model (New York: Springer, 1993).

22. Babcock, Green, and Robie, "Does Batterers' Treatment Work?" 1026.

23. Scott Raab, "Men Explode," Esquire 134, no. 3 (2000).

24. Miller, Victims as Offenders, 91–112.

25. For a recent review of research and thinking in this area, see Peter G. Jaffe et al., "Custody Disputes Involving Allegations of Domestic Violence: The Need for Differentiated Approaches to Parenting Plans," Family Court Review (forthcoming).

26. Donald G. Dutton, "Domestic Abuse Assessment in Child Custody Disputes: Beware the Domestic Violence Research Paradigm," Journal of Child Custody 2, no. 4 (2005); Donald G. Dutton, "On Comparing Apples with Apples Deemed Non-Existent: A Reply to Johnson," Journal of Child Custody 2, no. 4 (2005); Michael P. Johnson, "Apples and Oranges in Child Custody Disputes: Intimate Terrorism Vs. Situational Couple Violence," Journal of Child Custody 2, no. 4 (2005); Michael P. Johnson, "A Brief Reply to Dutton," Journal of Child Custody 2, no. 4 (2005).

27. Peter G. Jaffe, Claire V. Crooks, and Nick Bala, Making Appropriate Parenting Arrangements in Family Violence Cases: Applying the Literature to Identify Promising Practices (2005) (accessed June 21, 2007), available from http://www.justice.gc.ca/en/ps/pad/reports/2005-FCY-3/index.html; Janet R. Johnston, "A Child-Centered Approach to High-Conflict and Domestic-Violence Families: Differential Assessment and Interventions," Journal of Family Studies 12, no. 1 (2006); Janet R. Johnston and Joan B. Kelly, "Rejoinder to Gardner's 'Commentary on Kelly and Johnston's "The Alienated Child: A Reformulation of Parental Alienation Syndrome,"'" Family Court Review 42, no. (2004); Janet R. Johnston et al., "Allegations and Substantiations of Abuse in Cust

Disputing Families," Family Court Review 43, no. 2 (2005); Nancy ver Steegh, "Differentiating Types of Domestic Violence: Implications for Child Custody," Louisiana Law Review 65, no. 4 (2005).

28. Jaffe et al., recommend an assessment in terms of potency (severity of the violence), pattern (essentially a differentiation among the types I have discussed in this book), and primary perpetrator. Jaffe et al., "Custody Disputes."

29. Jaffe, Crooks, and Bala, Making Appropriate Parenting Arrangements.

30. Julia C. Babcock and Ramalina Steiner, "The Relationship between Treatment, Incarceration, and Recidivism of Battering: A Program Evaluation of Seattle's Coordinated Community Response to Domestic Violence," Journal of Family Psychology 13, no. 1 (1999); Melanie F. Shepard and Ellen L. Pence, eds., Coordinating Community Responses to Domestic Violence: Lessons from Duluth and Beyond (Thousand Oaks, Calif.: Sage, 1999).

31. Schechter, Women and Male Violence.

32. Theodora Ooms, Jacqueline Boggess, Anne Menard, Mary Myrick, Paula Roberts, Jack Tweedie, and Pamela Wilson, Building Bridges between Healthy Marriage, Responsible Fatherhood, and Domestic Violence Programs: A Preliminary Guide (Washington, D.C.: Center for Law and Social Policy, 2006).

Appendix A. Identifying Intimate Terrorism and Other Types of Partner Violence (pages 87–101)

1. Mary Ann Dutton and Lisa A. Goodman, "Coercion in Intimate Partner Violence: Toward a New Conceptualization," Sex Roles 52, no. 11/12 (2005).

2. Valerie Nash Chang, I Just Lost Myself: Psychological Abuse of Women in Marriage (Westport, Conn.: Praeger, 1996); K. Daniel O'Leary and Roland D. Maiuro, eds., Psychological Abuse in Violent Domestic Relations (New York: Springer, 2001); Richard M. Tolman, "Psychological Abuse of Women," Assessment of Family Violence: A Clinical and Legal Sourcebook, eds. Robert T. Ammerman and Michel Hersen (New York: John Wiley, 1992).

3. Mary Ann Dutton and Lisa Goodman, "Coercion and IPV: Development of a New Measure," paper presented at the International Conference on Family Violence (Durham, New Hampshire, 2005).

4. Ellen Pence and Michael Paymar, Education Groups for Men Who Batter: The Duluth Model (New York: Springer, 1993).

5. Nicola Graham-Kevan and John Archer, "Intimate Terrorism and Common Couple Violence: A Test of Johnson's Predictions in Four British Samples," Journal of Interpersonal Violence 18, no. 11 (2003); Nicola Graham-Kevan and John Archer, "Physical Aggression and Control in Heterosexual Relationships: The Effect of Sampling," Violence and Victims 18, no. 2 (2003); Nicola Graham-Kevan and John Archer, "Using Johnson's Domestic Violence Typology to Classify Men and Women in a Non-Selected Sample," unpublished, 2005.

6. Graham-Kevan and Archer, "Physical Aggression and Control."

7. Richard M. Tolman, "The Validation of the Psychological Maltreatment of Women Inventory," paper for the 4th International Family Violence Conference (Durham, New Hampshire, 1995); Richard M. Tolman, "The Development of a Measure of Psychological Maltreatment of Women by Their Male Partners" *Violence and Victims* 4, no. 3 (1989).

8. Holly Johnson, *Dangerous Domains: Violence against Women in Canada* (Toronto: Nelson Canada, 1996); Holly Johnson and Vincent F. Sacco, "Researching Violence against Women: Statistics Canada's National Survey," *Canadian Journal of Criminology* 37 (1995); Patricia Tjaden and Nancy Thoennes, "Extent, Nature, and Consequences of Intimate Partner Violence: Findings from the National Violence Against Women Survey"; Patricia Tjaden and Nancy Thoennes, *Violence and Threats of Violence against Women and Men in the United States, 1994–1996* (Ann Arbor, Mich.: Inter-university Consortium for Political and Social Research, 1999).

9. Michael P. Johnson, Valerie Conklin, and Nividetha Menon, "The Effects of Different Types of Domestic Violence on Women: Intimate Terrorism vs. Situational Couple Violence," paper presented at National Council on Family Relations annual meeting (Houston, Tex., 2002); Michael P. Johnson and Janel M. Leone, "The Differential Effects of Intimate Terrorism and Situational Couple Violence: Findings from the National Violence Against Women Survey," *Journal of Family Issues* 26, no. 3 (2005).

10. Irene Hanson Frieze and Maureen C. McHugh, "Power and Influence Strategies in Violent and Nonviolent Marriages," *Psychology of Women Quarterly* 16, no. 4 (1992): 172–73.

11. Irene Hanson Frieze and Angela Browne, "Violence in Marriage," in *Family Violence*, ed. Lloyd Ohlin and Michael Tonry, vol. 11, Crime and Justice: A Review of Research series (Chicago: University of Chicago Press, 1989).

12. Tjaden and Thoennes, "Extent, Nature, and Consequences of Intimate Partner Violence."

13. Johnson, *Dangerous Domains*.

14. Tolman, "The Development of a Measure."

15. Michael P. Johnson, "Conflict and Control: Symmetry and Asymmetry in Domestic Violence," in *Couples in Conflict*, eds. Alan Booth, Ann C. Crouter, and Mari Clements (Mahwah, N.J.: Lawrence Erlbaum, 2001); Michael P. Johnson, "Two Types of Violence against Women in the American Family: Identifying Patriarchal Terrorism and Common Couple Violence," paper presented at National Council on Family Relations annual meeting (Irvine, Calif., 1999).

16. Pence and Paymar, *The Duluth Model*.

17. Johnson, Conklin, and Menon, "The Effects of Different Types of Domestic Violence."

18. Johnson and Leone, "The Differential Effects of Intimate Terrorism and Situational Couple Violence"; Michael P. Johnson and Janel M. Leone, "The Differential Effects of Patriarchal Terrorism and Common Couple Violence: Findings from the National Violence against Women Survey," paper presented at the Tenth International

Conference on Personal Relationships (Brisbane, Australia, 2000). These papers are based on Janel Leone's master's thesis research: Janel M. Leone, "Factors Associated with Experiences of Patriarchal Terrorism and Common Couple Violence among Low-Income, Ethnic Women," master's thesis, Department of Individual and Family Studies, Pennsylvania State University (2000).

19. Janel M. Leone, Michael P. Johnson, Catherine M. Cohan, and Susan Lloyd, "Consequences of Different Types of Domestic Violence for Low-Income, Ethnic Women: A Control-Based Typology of Male-Partner Violence," paper presented at the International Network on Personal Relationships (Prescott, Ariz., June 2001). For another approach to the same data, see Janel M. Leone, Michael P. Johnson, Catherine M. Cohan, and Susan Lloyd, "Consequences of Male Partner Violence for Low-Income, Ethnic Women," *Journal of Marriage and Family* 66, no. 2 (2004).

20. Susan Lloyd, "The Effects of Domestic Violence on Women's Employment," *Law & Policy* 19, no. 2 (1997).

21. Murray A. Straus, "Measuring Intrafamily Conflict and Violence: The Conflict Tactics (CT) Scales," *Journal of Marriage & the Family* 41, no. 1 (1979).

22. Janel M. Leone, Michael P. Johnson, and Catherine L. Cohan, "Help-Seeking among Women in Violent Relationships: Factors Associated with Formal and Informal Help Utilization," paper presented at the National Council on Family Relations annual meeting (Vancouver, British Columbia, November 2003). For another approach to these data, see Janel M. Leone, Michael P. Johnson, and Catherine M. Cohan, "Victim Help-Seeking: Differences between Intimate Terrorism and Situational Couple Violence," *Family Relations* (forthcoming). These papers are based on Janel Leone's dissertation research: Janel M. Leone, "Help-Seeking among Women in Violent Relationships: Testing a Control-Based Typology of Partner Violence," Ph.D. dissertation, Department of Individual and Family Studies, The Pennsylvania State University, 2003.

23. Carolyn R. Block, *The Chicago Women's Health Risk Study: Risk of Serious Injury or Death in Intimate Violence*, Washington, D.C.: U.S. Department of Justice, National Institute of Justice, 2000.

24. D. Sheridan and W. Taylor, "Developing Hospital-Based Domestic Violence Programs, Protocol, Policies, and Procedures," *AWHONN's Clinical Issues* 4 (1993).

Appendix B. Stalking and
Separation-Precipitated Violence (pages 102–4)

1. Robert G. Lehnen and Wesley G. Skogan, *The National Crime Survey: Working Papers, Current and Historical Perspectives*," vol. 1, Washington, DC: U.S. Department of Justice, 1981.

2. Ronet Bachman and Linda E. Saltzman, *Violence against Women: Estimates from the Redesigned Survey*, special report, Washington, D.C.: U.S. Department of Justice, 1995.

3. Jacquelyn C. Campbell et al., "Risk Factors for Femicide in Abusive Relationships: Results from a Multisite Case Control Study," *American Journal of Public Health* 93,

no. 7 (2003): 1089. A recent review of the literature comes to much the same conclusion. Jacquelyn C. Campbell et al., "Intimate Partner Homicide: Review and Implications of Research and Policy," *Trauma Violence Abuse* 8, no. 3 (2007).

4. Holly Johnson and Tina Hotton, "Losing Control: Homicide Risk in Estranged and Intact Intimate Relationships," *Homicide Studies: An Interdisciplinary & International Journal* 7, no. 1 (2003): 71.

5. Brian H. Spitzberg and William R. Cupach, "The State of the Art of Stalking: Taking Stock of the Emerging Literature," *Aggression and Violent Behavior* 12, no. 1 (2007).

6. Janet R. Johnston and Linda E. Campbell, "A Clinical Typology of Interparental Violence in Disputed-Custody Divorces," *American Journal of Orthopsychiatry* 63, no. 2 (1993).

Appendix C. Gender and Intimate Partner Violence (pages 105–9)

1. Myra Marx Ferree, "Beyond Separate Spheres: Feminism and Family Research," *Journal of Marriage and the Family* 52, no. 4 (1990).

2. Myra Marx Ferree, Judith Lorber, and Beth B. Hess. "Introduction," in *Revisioning Gender*, eds. Myra Marx Ferree, Judith Lorber and Beth B. Hess (Walnut Creek, Calif.: AltaMira, 2000); Barbara Risman, "Gender as a Social Structure: Theory Wrestling with Activism," *Gender & Society* 18, no. 4 (2004).

3. Amy Holzworth-Munroe, Jeffrey C. Meehan, Katherine Herron, Uzma Rehman, and Gregory L. Stuart, "Testing the Holtzworth-Munroe and Stuart (1994) Batterer Typology," *Journal of Consulting and Clinical Psychology* 68, no. 6 (2000).

4. David B. Sugarman and Susan L. Frankel, "Patriarchal Ideology and Wife-Assault: A Meta-Analytic Review," *Journal of Family Violence* 11, no. 1 (1996).

5. Murray A. Straus, "The Controversy over Domestic Violence by Women: A Methodological, Theoretical, and Sociology of Science Analysis," in *Violence in Intimate Relationships*, ed. Ximena B. Arriaga and Stuart Oskamp (Thousand Oaks, Calif.: Sage, 1999).

6. Suzanne C. Swan and David L. Snow, "A Typology of Women's Use of Violence in Intimate Relationships," *Violence against Women* 8, no. 3 (2002).

7. R. Emerson Dobash and Russell P. Dobash, *Violence against Wives: A Case against Patriarchy* (New York: Free Press, 1979); R. Emerson Dobash and Russell P. Dobash, *Women, Violence and Social Change* (New York: Routledge, 1992); Kersti Yllö and Michele Bograd, editors, *Feminist Perspectives on Wife Abuse* (Newbury Park, Calif.: Sage, 1988).

8. Renate C. A. Klein and Robert M. Milardo, "The Social Context of Couple Conflict: Support and Criticism from Informal Third Parties," *Journal of Social and Personal Relationships* 17, no. 4–5 (2000).

9. Eva Schlesinger Buzawa, *Domestic Violence: The Criminal Justice Response* (Thousand Oaks, Calif.: Sage, 2003).

10. R. Emerson Dobash and Russell P. Dobash, *Women, Violence and Social Change* (New York: Routledge, 1992); Evan Stark, *Coercive Control: The Entrapment of Women in Personal Life* (New York: Oxford University Press, 2007).

11. James Alan Fox and Marianne W. Zawitz, "Homicide Trends in the United States," United States Department of Justice, http://www.ojp.usdoj.gov/bjs/homicide/ homtrnd.htm (accessed July 6, 2007); Callie Marie Rennison, *Intimate Partner Violence, 1993–2001* (Washington, D.C.: U.S. Department of Justice, Bureau of Justice Statistics, 2003).

12. Suzanne K. Steinmetz, "The Battered Husband Syndrome," *Victimology* 2, no. 3–4 (1977–78).

13. John Archer, "Sex Differences in Aggression between Heterosexual Partners: A Meta-Analytic Review," *Psychological Bulletin* 126, no. 5 (2000); Lisa D. Brush, "Violent Acts and Injurious Outcomes in Married Couples: Methodological Issues in the National Survey of Families and Households," *Gender & Society* 4, no. 1 (1990); L. Kevin Hamberger and Clare E. Guse, "Men's and Women's Use of Intimate Partner Violence in Clinical Samples," *Violence against Women* 8, no. 11 (2002); Michael P. Johnson, "Two Types of Violence against Women in the American Family: Identifying Patriarchal Terrorism and Common Couple Violence," paper presented at National Council on Family Relations annual meeting (Irvine, Calif.: 1999); Barbara J. Morse, "Beyond the Conflict Tactics Scale: Assessing Gender Differences in Partner Violence," *Violence and Victims* 10, no. 4 (1995); Patricia Tjaden and Nancy Thoennes, "Prevalence and Consequences of Male-to-Female and Female-to-Male Intimate Partner Violence as Measured by the National Violence Against Women Survey," *Violence against Women* 6, no. 2 (2000).

14. Michael P. Johnson, "Gendered Communication and Intimate Partner Violence," in *The Sage Handbook of Gender and Communication* eds. Bonnie J. Dow and Julia T. Wood (Thousand Oaks, Calif.: Sage, 2006).

15. Claire M. Renzetti, editor's note in "Women's Use of Violence in Intimate Relationships," part 2, special issue, *Violence against Women* 8, no. 12 (2002); Claire M. Renzetti, *Violent Betrayal: Partner Abuse in Lesbian Relationships* (Thousand Oaks, Calif.: Sage, 1992); Claire M. Renzetti and Charles Harvey Miley, editors, *Violence in Gay and Lesbian Domestic Partnerships* (New York: Haworth Press, 1996).

References

Aguilar, Rudy J., and Narina Nunez Nightengale. "The Impact of Specific Battering Experience on the Self-Esteem of Abused Women." *Journal of Family Violence* 9, no. 1 (1994): 35–45.

Ammon, Linda L. "Dealing with the Nastiness: Mixing Feminism and Criminal Law in the Review of Cases of Battered Incarcerated Women—A Tenth-Year Reflection." *Buffalo Criminal Law Review* 4 (2001): 891–916.

Archer, John. "Sex Differences in Aggression between Heterosexual Partners: A Meta-Analytic Review." *Psychological Bulletin* 126, no. 5 (2000): 651–80.

Athens, Lonnie H. *Violent Criminal Acts and Actors Revisited.* Chicago: University of Illinois Press, 1997.

Babcock, Julia C., Charles E. Green, and Chet Robie. "Does Batterers' Treatment Work? A Meta-Analytic Review of Domestic Violence Treatment." *Clinical Psychology Review* 23, no. 8 (2004): 1023–53.

Babcock, Julia C., and Ramalina Steiner. "The Relationship between Treatment, Incarceration, and Recidivism of Battering: A Program Evaluation of Seattle's Coordinated Community Response to Domestic Violence." *Journal of Family Psychology* 13, no. 1 (1999): 46–59.

Bachman, Ronet, and Dianne Cyr Carmody. "Fighting Fire with Fire: The Effects of Victim Resistance in Intimate Versus Stranger Perpetrated Assaults against Females." *Journal of Family Violence* 9, no. 4 (1994): 317–31.

Bachman, Ronet, and Linda E. Saltzman. *Violence against Women: Estimates from the Redesigned Survey.* Special Report Washington, D.C.: U.S. Department of Justice, 1995.

Block, Carolyn R. *The Chicago Women's Health Risk Study: Risk of Serious Injury or Dealth in Intimate Violence.* Washington, D.C.: U.S. Department of Justice, National Institute of Justice, 2000.

Bradbury, Thomas, Ronald Rogge, and Erika Lawrence. "Reconsidering the Role of Conflict in Marriage." In *Couples in Conflict*, edited by Alan Booth, Ann C. Crouter, and Mari Clements, 59–81. Mahwah, N.J.: Lawrence Erlbaum Associates, 2001.

Browne, Angela. *When Battered Women Kill.* New York: Free Press, 1987.

Browne, Angela, Kirk R. Williams, and Donald G. Duggon. "Homicide between Intimate Partners: A 20-Year Review." In *Homicide: A Sourcebook of Social Research*, edited by M. Dwayne Smith and Margaret A. Zahn, 149–64. Thousand Oaks, Calif.: Sage, 1999.

Brush, Lisa D. "Violent Acts and Injurious Outcomes in Married Couples: Methodological Issues in the National Survey of Families and Households." *Gender & Society* 4, no. 1 (1990): 56–67.

Burgess-Proctor, Amanda K. "Evaluating the Efficacy of Protection Orders for Victims of Domestic Violence." *Women and Criminal Justice* 15 (2003): 33–54.

Burke, Jessica G., Andrea Carlson Gielen, Karen A. McDonnell, Patricia O'Campo, and Suzanne Maman. "The Process of Ending Abuse in Intimate Relationships: A Qualitative Exploration of the Transtheoretical Model." *Violence Against Women* 7, no. 10 (2001): 1144–63.

Buzawa, Eva Schlesinger. *Domestic Violence: The Criminal Justice Response.* Thousand Oaks, Calif.: Sage, 2003.

Buzawa, Eve Schlesinger, and Carl G. Buzawa, eds. *Do Arrests and Restraining Orders Work?* Edited by Eve Schlesinger Buzawa and Carl G. Buzawa. Thousand Oaks, Calif.: Sage Publications, Inc., 1996.

Campbell, Jacquelyn C. "Making the Health Care System an Empowerment Zone for Battered Women: Health Consequences, Policy Recommendations, Introduction, and Overview." In *Empowering Survivors of Abuse: Health Care for Battered Women and Their Children,* edited by Jacquelyn C. Campbell, 3–22. Thousand Oaks, Calif.: Sage, 1998.

———. "Prediction of Homicide of and by Battered Women." In *Assessing Dangerousness: violence by Sexual Offenders, Batterers, and Child Abusers,* edited by Jacquelyn C. Campbell. Thousand Oaks, Calif.: Sage, 1995.

———, ed. *Assessing Dangerousness: Violence by Sexual Offenders, Batterers, and Child Abusers.* Thousand Oaks, Calif.: Sage, 1998.

———, ed. *Empowering Survivors of Abuse: health Care for Battered Women and Their Children.* Thousand Oaks, Calif.: Sage, 1998.

Campbell, Jacquelyn C., N. Glass, P. W. Sharps, K. Laughon, and T. Bloom. "Intimate Partner Homicide: Review and Implications of Research and Policy." *Trauma Violence Abuse* 8, no. 3 (2007): 246–69.

Campbell, Jacquelyn C., Linda Rose, Joan Kub, and Daphne Nedd. "Voices of Strength and Resistance: A Contextual and Longitudinal Analysis of Women's Responses to Battering." *Journal of Interpersonal Violence* 13, no. 6 (1998): 743–62.

Campbell, Jacquelyn C., and Karen L. Soeken. "Forced Sex and Intimate Partner Violence: Effects on Women's Risk and Women's Health." *Violence Against Women* 5, no. 9 (1999): 1017–35.

Campbell, Jacquelyn C., D. Webster, J. Koziol-McLain, C. Block, D. Campbell, M. A. Curry, F. Gary, N. Glass, J. McFarlane, C. Sachs, P. Sharps, Y. Ulrich, S. A. Wilt, J. Manganello, X. Xu, J. Schollenberger, V. Frye, and K. Laughon. "Risk Factors for Femicide in Abusive Relationships: Results from a Multisite Case Control Study." *American Journal of Public Health* 93, no. 7 (2003: 1089–97.

Campbell, Jacquelyn C., Anne B. Woods, Kathryn Laughon Chouaf, and Barbara Parker. "Reproductive Health Consequences of Intimate Partner Violence: A Nursing Research Review." *Clinical Nursing Research* 9, no. 3 (2000): 217–37.

Cascardi, Michele, and K. Daniel O'Leary. "Depressive Symptomology, Self-Esteem, and Self-Blame in Battered Women" *Journal of Family Violence* 7, no. 4 (1992): 249–59.

Chang, Valerie Nash. *I Just Lost Myself: Psychological Abuse of Women in Marriage.* Westport, Conn.: Praeger, 1996.

Clements, Kahni, Amy Holtzworth-Munroe, Edward W. Gondolf, and Jeffrey C. Meehan. "Testing the Holtzworth-Monroe Et Al. (2000) Batterer Typology among Court-Referred Maritally Violent Men." Paper presented at the Association for the Advancement of Behavior Therapy annual meeting, Reno, Nevada, November 2002.

Cramer, Elizabeth P. "Unintended Consequences of Constructing Criminal Justice as a Dominant Paradigm in Understanding and Intervening in Intimate Partner Violence." *Women's Studies Quarterly* 33, no. 1/2 (2005): 1–2.

Davies, Jill, Eleanor Lyon, and Diane Monti-Catania. *Safety Planning with Battered Women: Complex Lives/Difficult Choices.* Thousand Oaks, Calif.: Sage, 1998.

DeJong, Christiana, and Amanda K. Burgess-Proctor. "A Summary of Personal Protection Order Statutes in the United States." *Violence Against Women* 12, no. 1 (2006): 68–88.

DeMaris, Alfred, and Steven Swinford. "Female Victims of Spousal Violence: Factors Influencing Their Level of Fearfulness." *Family Relations* 45 (1996): 98–106.

Dobash, R. Emerson, and Russell P. Dobash. *Violence against Wives: A Case against Patriarchy.* New York: Free Press, 1979.

———. *Women, Violence and Social Change.* New York: Routledge, 1992.

Dobash, Russell P., R. Emerson Dobash, Margo Wilson, and Martin Daly. "The Myth of Sexual Symmetry in Marital Violence." *Social Problems* 39, no. 1 (1992): 71–91.

Dutton, Donald G. *The Batterer: A Psychological Profile.* New York: Basic Books, 1995.

———. "Domestic Abuse Assessment in Child Custody Disputes: Beware the Domestic Violence Research Paradigm." *Journal of Child Custody* 2, no. 4 (2005): 23–42.

———. "On Comparing Apples with Apples Deemed Non-Existent: A Reply to Johnson." *Journal of Child Custody* 2, no. 4 (2005): 53–63.

Dutton, Mary Ann, and Lisa Goodman. "Coercion and IPV: Development of a New Measure." Paper presented at the International Conference on Family Violence, Durham, New Hampshire, 2005.

Dutton, May Ann, and Lisa A Goodman. "Coercion in Intimate Partner Violence: Toward a New Conceptualization." *Sex Roles* 52, no. 11/12 (2005): 743–57.

———. Personal Communication, May 2002.

Eckhardt, Christopher I., Amy Holtzworth-Munroe, B. Nedander, A. Sibley, I. Tegun, and M. Cahill. "Readiness to Change, Partner Violence Subtypes, and Treatment Outcomes among Men in Treatment for Partner Assault." *Violence and Victims*, in press.

Feldman, Clyde M., and Carl A. Ridley. "The Role of Conflict-Based Communication Responses and Outcomes in Male Domestic Violence toward Female Partners." *Journal of Social and Personal Relationships* 17, no. 4–5 (2000): 552–73.

Felson, Richard B. *Violence and Gender Reexamined*. Washington, D.C.: American Psychological Association, 2002.

Felson, Richard B., and Steven F. Messner. "The Control Motive in Intimate Partner Violence." *Social Psychology Quarterly* 63, no. 1 (2000): 86–94.

Ferraro, Kathleen J. "Battered Women: Strategies for Survival." In *Violence among Intimate Partners: Patterns, Causes and Effects*, edited by Albert P. Carderelli, 124–40. New York: Macmillan, 1997.

———. "The Dance of Dependency: A Genealogy of Domestic Violence Discourse." *Hypatia* 11, no. 4 (1996): 77–91.

Ferree, Myra Marx. "Beyond Separate spheres: Feminism and Family Research." *Journal of Marriage and the Family* 52, no. 4 (1990): 866–84.

Ferree, Myra Marx, Judith Lorber, and Beth B. Hess. Introduction. In *Revisioning Gender*, edited by Myra Marx Ferree, Judith Lorber and Beth B. Hess, xv–xxxvi. Walnut Creek, Calif.: AltaMira, 2000.

Fox, James Alan, and Marianne W. Zawitz. *Homicide Trends in the United States*. Bureau of Justice Statistics, United States Department of Justice (June 29, 2006). Available at http://www.ojp.usdoj.gov/bjs/homicide/homtrnd.htm (accessed July 6, 2007).

Frieze, Irene Hanson, and Angela Browne. "Violence in Marriage." In *Family Violence*, edited by Lloyd Ohlin and Michael Tonry, 163–218. Chicago: University of Chicago Press, 1989.

Frieze, Irene Hanson, and Maureen C. McHugh. "Power and Influence Strategies in Violent and Nonviolent Marriages." *Psychology of Women Quarterly* 16, no. 4 (1992): 449–65.

Gelles, Richard J. "Violence in the Family: A Review of Research in the Seventies." *Journal of Marriage & the Family* 42, no. 4 (1980).

———. *The Violent Home*. Newbury Park, Calif.: Sage, 1987 [1974].

Gelles, Richard J., and Murray A. Straus. "Determinants of Violence in the Family: Toward a Theoretical Integration." In *Contemporary Theories About the Family*, edited by Wesley Burr, Reuben Hill, F. Ivan Nye, and Ira Reiss, 549–81. New York: Free Press, 1979.

———. *Intimate Violence: The Causes and Consequences of Abuse in the American Family*. New York: Simon & Schuster, 1988.

Golding, Jacqueline M. "Intimate Partner violence as a Risk Factor for Mental Disorders: A Meta-Analysis." *Journal of Family Violence* 14, no. 2 (1999): 99–132.

Gondolf, Edward W. "Who Are Those Guys? Toward a Behavioral Typology of Batterers." *Violence and Victims* 3, (Fall 1988): 187–203.

Gondolf, Edward W., and Ellen R. Fisher. *Battered Women as Survivors: An Alternative to Treating Learned Helplessness*. Lexington, Mass.: D.C. Heath, 1988.

Graham-Kevan, Nicola, and John Archer. "Intimate Terrorism and Common Couple Violence: A Test of Johnson's Predictions in Four British Samples." *Journal of Interpersonal Violence* 18, no. 11 (2003): 1247–70.

———. "Physical Aggression and Control in Heterosexual Relationships: The Effect of Sampling." *Violence and Victims* 18, no. 2 (2003): 181–96.

———. "Using Johnson's Domestic Violence Typology to Classify Men and Women in an Non-Selected Sample." Unpublished, 2005.

Grandin, Elaine, Eugen Lupri, and Merlin B. Brinkerhoff. "Couple Violence and Psychological Distress." *Canadian Journal of Public Health* 89, no. 1 (1998): 43–47.

Hamberger, L. Kevin, and Clare E. Guse. "Men's and Women's Use of Intimate Partner Violence in Clinical Samples." *Violence against Women* 8, no. 11 (2002): 1301–31.

Hargovan, Hema. "Restorative Justice and Domestic Violence: Some Exploratory Thoughts." *Agenda* 66 (2005): 48–56.

Holtzworth-Munroe, Amy. "A Typology of Men Who Are Violent toward Their Female Partners: Making Sense of the Heterogeneity in Husband Violence." *Current Directions in Psychological Science* 9, no. 4 (2000): 140–43.

Holtzworth-Munroe, Amy, Jeffrey C. Meehan, Katherine Herron, Uzma Rehman, and Gregory L. Stuart. "Do Subtypes of Martially Violent Men Continue to Differ over Time?" *Journal of Consulting and Clinical Psychology* 71, no. 4 (2003): 728–40.

———. "Testing the Holtzworth-Munroe and Stuart (1994) Batterer Typology." *Journal of Consulting and Clinical Psychology* 68 (2000): 1000–19.

Holtzworth-Munroe, Amy, Jeffrey C. Meehan, Katherine Herron, and Gregory L. Stuart. "A Typology of Male Batterers: An Initial Examination." In *Violence in Intimate Relationships*, edited by Ximena B. Arriaga and Stuart Oskamp, 45–72. Thousand Oaks, Calif.: Sage, 1999.

Holtzworth-Munroe, Amy, and Gregory L. Stuart. "Typologies of Male Batterers: Three Subtypes and the Differences among Them." *Psychological Bulletin* 116, no. 3 (1994): 476–97.

Hotaling, Gerald T., and David B. Sugarman. "An Analysis of Risk Markers in Husband to Wife Violence: The Current State of Knowledge." *Violence & Victims* 1 (1986): 101–24.

Infante, Dominic A., Teresa A. Chandler, and Jill E. Rudd. "Test of an Argumentative Skill Deficiency Model of Interspousal Violence." *Communication Monographs* 56, no. 2 (1989): 163–77.

Infante, Dominic A., Scott A. Myers, and Rick A. Buerkel. "Argument and Verbal Aggression in Constructive and Destructive Family and Organizational Disagreements." *Western Journal of Communication* 58, no. 2 (1994): 73–84.

Infante, Dominic A., and Andrew S. Rancer. "Argumentativeness and Verbal Aggressiveness: A Review of Recent Theory and Research." In *Communication Yearbook 1996*, edited by Brant R. Burleson, 319–51. Thousand Oaks, Calif.: Sage, 1996.

Infante, Dominic A., and C. J. Wigley. "Verbal Aggressiveness: An Interpersonal Model and Measure." *Communication Monographs* 53, no. 1 (1986): 61–69.

Jacobson, Neil S., and John M. Gottman. *When Men Batter Women: New Insights into Ending Abusive Relationships.* New York: Simon & Schuster, 1998.

Jacobson, Neil S., John M. Gottman, Jennifer Waltz, Regina Rushe, Julia Babcock, and Amy Holtzworth-Munroe. "Affect, Verbal Content, and Psychophysiology in the Arguments of Couples with a Violent Husband." *Journal of Consulting and Clinical Psychology* 62, no. 5 (1994): 982–88.

Jaffe, Peter G., Claire V. Crooks, and Nick Bala. *Making Appropriate Parenting Arrangements in Family Violence Cases: Applying the Literature to Identify Promising Practices.* Canada Department of Justice, 2005. http://www.justice.gc.ca/en/ps/pad/reports/2005-FCY-3/index.html (accessed June 21, 2007).

Jaffe, Peter G., Janet R. Johnston, Claire V. Crooks, and Nick Bala. "Custody Disputes Involving Allegations of Domestic Violence: The Need for Differentiated Approaches to Parenting Plans." *Family Court Review* (in press).

Jang, Deeana L., Leni Martin, and Gail Pendleton. "Domestic Violence in Immigrant and Refugee Communities: Asserting the Rights of Battered Women." Washington, D.C.: Family Violence Prevention Fund, 1997.

Jasinski, Jana L., and Linda M. Williams, eds. *Partner Violence: A Comprehensive Review of 20 Years of Research.* Thousand Oaks, Calif.: Sage, 1998.

Johnson, Holly. *Dangerous Domains: Violence against Women in Canada.* Toronto: Nelson Canada, 1996.

Johnson, Holly, and Tina Hotton. "Losing Control: Homicide Risk in Estranged and Intact Intimate Relationships." *Homicide Studies: An Interdisciplinary & International Journal* 7, no. 1 (2003): 58–84.

Johnson, Holly, and Vincent F. Sacco. "Researching Violence against Women: Statistics Canada's National Survey." *Canadian Journal of Criminology* 37 (1995): 281–304.

Johnson, Michael P. "Apples and Oranges in Child Custody Disputes: Intimate Terrorism Vs. Situational Couple Violence." *Journal of Child Custody* 2, no. 4 (2005): 43–52.

———. Review of *Restorative Justice and Family Violence*, ed. Heather Strang and John Braithwaite. *Contemporary Sociology: A Journal of Reviews* 33, no. 1 (2004): 96–98.

———. "A Brief Reply to Dutton." *Journal of Child Custody* 2, no. 4 (2005): 65–67.

———. "Conflict and Control: Gender Symmetry and Asymmetry in Domestic Violence." *Violence against Women* 12, no. 11 (2006): 1–16.

———. "Conflict and Control: Symmetry and Asymmetry in Domestic Violence." In *Couples in Conflict*, edited by Alan Booth, Ann C. Crouter, and Mari Clements, 95–104. Mahwah, N.J.: Lawrence Erlbaum, 2001.

———. "Domestic Violence: The Intersection of Gender and Control." In *Gender Violence: Interdisciplinary Perspectives*, 2nd ed., edited by Laura L. O'Toole, Jessica R. Schiffman, and Margie Kiter Edwards, 257–68. New York: New York University Press, 2007.

———. "Gendered Communication and Intimate Partner Violence." In *The Sage

Handbook of Gender and Communication, edited by Bonnie J. Dow and Julia T. Wood, 71–87. Thousand Oaks, Calif.: Sage, 2006.

———. "Patriarchal Terrorism and Common Couple Violence: Two Forms of Violence against Women." *Journal of Marriage and the Family* 57, no. 2 (1995): 283–94.

———. "Two Types of Violence against Women in the American Family: Identifying Patriarchal Terrorism and Common Couple Violence." Paper presented at the National Council on Family Relations annual meeting, Irvine, California, 1999.

Johnson, Michael P., and Alison Cares. "Effects and Non-Effects of Childhood Experiences of Family Violence on Adult Partner Violence." Paper presented at the National Council on Family Relations annual meeting, Orlando, Florida, 2004.

Johnson, Michael P., Valerie Conklin, and Nividetha Menon. "The Effects of Different Types of Domestic Violence on Women: Intimate Terrorism Vs. Situational Couple Violence." Paper presented at the National Council on Family Relations annual meeting, Houston, Texas, 2002.

Johnson, Michael P., and Kathleen J. Ferraro. "Research on Domestic Violence in the 1990s: Making Distinctions." *Journal of Marriage and the Family* 62, no. 4 (2000): 948–63.

Johnson, Michael P., and Janel M. Leone. "The Differential Effects of Intimate Terrorism and Situational Couple Violence: Findings from the National Violence Against Women Survey." *Journal of Family Issues* 26, no. 3 (2005): 322–49.

———. "The Differential Effects of Patriarchal Terrorism and Common Couple Violence: Findings from the National Violence against Women Survey." Paper presented at the Tenth International Conference on Personal Relationships, Brisbane, Australia, 2000.

Johnston, Janet R. "A Child-Centered Approach to High-Conflict and Domestic-Violence Families: Differential Assessment and Interventions." *Journal of Family Studies* 12, no. 1 (2006): 15–35.

Johnsoton, Janet R., and Linda E. Campbell. "A Clinical Typology of Interparental Violence in Disputed-Custody Divorces." *American Journal of Orthopsychiatry* 63, no. 2 (1993): 190–99.

Johnston, Janet R., and Joan B. Kelly. "Rejoinder to Gardner's 'Commentary on Kelly and Johnston's "The Alienated Child: A Reformulation of Parental Alienation Syndrome."'" *Family Court Review* 42, no. 4 (2004): 622–28.

Johnston, Janet R. Soyoung Lee, Nancy W. Olesen, and Marjorie G. Walters. "Allegations and Substantiations of Abuse in Custody-Disputing Families." *Family Court Review* 43, no. 2 (2005): 283–94.

Jones, Ann. *Women Who Kill*. Boston: Beacon Press, 1996.

Kantor, Glenda Kaufman, and Jana L. Jasinski. "Dynamics and Risk Factors in Partner Violence." In *Partner Violence*, edited by Jasinski and Williams, 1–43.

Kantor, Glenda Kaufman, and Murray A. Straus. "The 'Drunken Bum' Theory of Wife Beating." In *Physical Violence in American Families*, edited by Straus and Gelles, 203–24.

Kelley, Harold H., Ellen Berscheid, Andrew Christiansen, John H. Harvey, Ted L. Huston, George Levinger, Evie McClintock, Letitia Anne Peplau, and Donald R. Peterson. *Close Relationships*. New York: W. H. Freeman, 1983.

Kimmel, Michael S. "'Gender Symmetry' in Domestic Violence: A Substantive and Methodological Research Review." *Violence Against Women* 8, no. 11 (2002): 1332–63.

Kirkwood, Catherine. *Leaving Abusive Partners: From the Scars of Survival to the Wisdom for Change*. Newbury Park, Calif.: Sage, 1993.

Kleckner, James H. "Wife Beaters and Beaten Wives: Co-Conspirators in Crimes of Violence." *Psychology: A Journal of Human Behavior* 15, no. 1 (1978): 54–56.

Klein, Renate C. A., and Robert M. Milardo. "The Social Context of Couple Conflict: Support and Criticism from Informal Third Parties." *Journal of Social and Personal Relationships* 17, no. 4–5 (2000): 618–37.

Kurz, Demie. "Social Science Perspectives on Wife Abuse: Current Debates and Future Directions." *Gender & Society* 3, no. 4 (1989): 489–505.

Laroche, Denis. *Aspects of the Context and Consequences of Domestic Violence: Situational Couple Violence and Intimate Terrorism in Canada*. Government of Quebec: Institut de la statistique du Québec, Québec, 2005.

Lehnen, Robert G., and Wesley G. Skogan. *The National Crime Survey: Working Papers, Current and Historical Perspectives*. Vol. 1. Washington, D.C.: U.S. Department of Justice, 1981.

Leone, Janel M. "Factors Associated with Experiences of Patriarchal Terrorism and Common Couple Violence among Low-Income, Ethnic Women." Master's thesis, Department of Individual and Family Studies, Pennsylvania State University 2000.

———. "Help-Seeking among Women in Violent Relationships: Testing a Control-Based Typology of Partner Violence." PhD diss., Department of Individual and Family Studies, Pennsylvania State University, 2003.

Leone, Janel M., Michael P. Johnson, and Catherine L. Cohan. "Help-Seeking among Women in Violent Relationships: Factors Associated with Formal and Informal Help Utilization." Paper presented at the National Council on Family Relations annual meeting, Vancouver, British Columbia, November 2003.

———. "Victim Help-Seeking: Differences between Intimate Terrorism and Situational Couple Violence." *Family Relations* 56, no. 5 (2007): 427–39.

Leone, Janel M., Michael P. Johnson, Catherine M. Cohan, and Susan Lloyd. "Consequences of Different Types of Domestic Violence for Low-Income, Ethnic Women: A Control-Based Typology of Male-Partner Violence." Paper presented at the International Network on Personal Relationships, Prescott, Arizona, June 2001.

———. "Consequences of Male Partner Violence for Low-Income, Ethnic Women." *Journal of Marriage and Family* 66, no. 2 (2004): 471–89.

Leventhal, Beth, and Sandra E. Lundy, eds. *Same-Sex Domestic Violence: Strategies for Change.* Thousand Oaks, Calif.: Sage, 1999.

Lloyd, Susan. "The Effects of Domestic Violence on Women's Employment" *Law & Policy* 19, no. 2 (1997): 139–67.

Lloyd, Susan, and Nina Taluc. "The Effects of Male Violence on Female Employment." *Violence Against Women* 5, no. 4 (1999): 370–92.

Macmillan, Ross, and Rosemary Gartner. "When She Brings Home the Bacon: Labor-Force Participation and the Risk of Spousal Violence against Women." *Journal of Marriage and the Family* 61, no. 4 (1999): 947–58.

Magdol, Lynn, Terrie E. Moffitt, Avshalom Caspi, Denise L. Newman, Jeffrey Fagan, and Phil A. Silva. "Gender Differences in Partner Violence in a Birth Cohort of 21-Year-Olds: Bridging the Gap between Clinical and Epidemiological Approaches." *Journal of Consulting & Clinical Psychology* 65, no. 1 (1997): 68–78.

Martin, Dell. *Battered Wives.* New York: Pocket Books, 1976.

Merritt-Gray, Marilyn, and Judith Wuest. "Counteracting Abuse and Breaking Free: The Process of Leaving Revealed through Women's Voices." *Health Care for Women International* 16, no. 5 (1995): 399–412.

Miller, Susan L. *Victims as Offenders: The Paradox of Women's Violence in Relationships.* New Brunswick, N.J.: Rutgers, 2005.

Mills, Linda G. *Insult to Injury: Rethinking Our Responses to Intimate Abuse.* Princeton, N.J.: Princeton University Press, 2003.

Morse, Barbara J. "Beyond the Conflict Tactics Scale: Assessing Gender Differences in Partner Violence." *Violence and Victims* 10, no. 4 (1995): 251–72.

O'Leary, K. Daniel, and Roland D. Maiuro, eds. *Psychological Abuse in Violent Domestic Relations.* New York: Springer, 2001.

Olson, Loreen. "Exploring 'Common Couple Violence' in Heterosexual Romantic Relationships." *Western Journal of Communication* 66, no. 1 (2002): 104–128.

Ooms, Theodora, Jacqueline Boggess, Anne Menard, Mary Myrick, Paula Roberts, Jack Tweedie, and Pamela Wilson. *Building Bridges between Healthy Marriage, Responsible Fatherhood, and Domestic Violence Programs: A Preliminary Guide.* Washington, D.C.: Center for Law and Social Policy, 2006.

Orava, Tammy., Peter J. McLeod, and Donald Sharp. "Perceptions of Control, Depressive Symptomatology, and Self-Esteem of Women in Transition from Abusive Relationships." *Journal of Family Violence* 11, no. 2 (1996): 167–86.

Pagelow, Mildred Daley. *Woman-Battering: Victims and Their Experiences.* Newbury Park, Calif.: Sage, 1981.

Pasley, Kay, Jennifer Kerpelman, and Douglas E. Guilbert. "Gendered Conflict, Identity Disruption, and Marital Instability: Expanding Gottman's Model." *Journal of Social and Personal Relationships* 18, no. 1 (2001): 5–27.

Pence, Ellen, and Michael Paymar. *Education Groups for Men Who Batter: The Duluth Model.* New York: Springer, 1993.

Pleck, Elizabeth, Joseph H. Pleck, Marlyn Grossman, and Pauline B. Bart. "The Battered Data Syndrome: A Comment on Steinmetz' Article." *Victimology* 2 (1978): 680–83.

Presser, Lois, and Emily Gaarder. "Can Restorative Justice Reduce Battering? Some Preliminary Considerations." *Social Justice* 27, no. 1 (2000): 175–95.

Raab, Scott. "Men Explode." *Esquire* 134, no. 3 (2000): 244ff.

Rennison, Callie Marie. *Intimate Partner Violence, 1993–2001.* Special report. U.S. Department of Justice, Bureau of Justice Statistics, 2003.

Renzetti, Claire M. Editor's note, "Women's Use of Violence in Intimate Relationships." Special issue, part 2. *Violence against Women* 8, no. 12 (2002): 1419.

———. *Violent Betrayal: Partner Abuse in Lesbian Relationships.* Thousand Oaks, Calif.: Sage, 1992.

Renzetti, Claire M., and Charles Harvey Miley. *Violence in Gay and Lesbian Domestic Partnerships.* New York: Haworth Press, 1996.

Richie, Beth. *Compelled to Crime: The Gender Entrapment of Battered Black Women.* New York: Routledge, 1996.

Ridley, Carl A., and Clyde M. Feldman. "Female Domestic Violence toward Male Partners: Exploring Conflict Responses and Outcomes." *Journal of Family Violence* 18, no. 3 (2003): 157–70.

Riger, Stephanie, Courtney Ahrens, and Amy Blinkenstaff. "Measuring Interference with Employment and Education Reported by Women with Abusive Partners: Preliminary Data." In *Psychological Abuse in Violent Domestic Relations,* edited by O'Leary and Maiuro, 119–33.

Risman, Barbara. "Gender as a Social Structure: Theory Wrestling with Activism." *Gender & Society* 18, no.4 (2004): 429–50.

Roloff, Michael E. "The Catalyst Hypothesis: Conditions under Which Coercive Communication Leads to Physical Aggression." In *Family Violence from a Communication Perspective,* edited by Dudley D. Cahn and Sally A. Lloyd, 20–36. Thousand Oaks, Calif.: Sage, 1996.

Ross, L.E. "Do Arrests and Restraining Orders Work?" *International Journal of Offender Therapy and Comparative Criminology* 42, no. 2 (1998): 181–83.

Roy, Maria, ed. *Battered Women: A Psychosociological Study of Domestic Violence.* New York: Van Nostrand Reinhold, 1977.

Russell, Diana E. *Rape in Marriage.* New York: Collier Books, 1982.

Russo, Nancy Felipe, J.E. Denious, G.P. Keita, and Mary P. Koss. "Intimate Violence and Black Women's Health." *Women's Health* 3, no. 3–4 (1997): 315–48.

Sabourin, Teresa Chandler. "The Role of Communication in Verbal Abuse between Partners." In *Family Violence from a Communication Perspective,* edited by Dudley D. Cahn and Sally A. Lloyd, 199–217. Thousand Oaks, Calif.: Sage 1996.

———. "The Role of Negativity Reciprocity in Spouse Abuse: A Relational Control Analysis." *Journal of Applied Communication Research* 23, no. 4 (1995): 271–83.

Sackett, Leslie A., and Daniel G. Saunders. "The Impact of Different Forms of Psychological Abuse on Battered Women." *Violence and Victims* 14, no. 1 (1999): 105–17.

Saunders, Daniel G. "Are Physical Assaults by Wives and Girlfriends a Major Social Problem? A review of the Literature." *Violence against Women* 8, no. 12 (2002): 1424–48.

———. "Feminist-Cognitive-Behavioral and Process-Psychodynamic Treatments for Men Who Batter: Interactions of Abuser Traits and Treatment Model." *Violence and Victims* 4, no. 4 (1996): 393–414.

———. "Posttraumatic Stress Symptom Profiles of Battered Women: A Comparison of Survivors in Two Settings." *Violence and Victims* 9, no. 1 (1994): 31–44.

———. "A Typology of Men Who Batter: Three Types Derived from Cluster Analysis." *American Journal of Orthopsychiatry* 62, no. 2 (1992): 264–75.

Schechter, Susan. *Women and Male Violence: The Visions and Struggles of the Battered Women's Movement.* Boston: South End Press, 1982.

Shainess, Natalie. "Vulnerability to Violence: Masochism as Process." *American Journal of Psychotherapy* 33, no. 2 (1979): 174–89.

Shepard, Melanie F., and Ellen L. Pence, eds. *Coordinating Community Responses to Domestic Violence: Lessons from Duluth and Beyond.* Thousand Oaks, Calif.: Sage, 1999.

Sheridan, D., and W. Taylor. "Developing Hospital-Based Domestic Violence Programs, Protocol, Policies, and Procedures." *AWHONN's Clinical Issues* 4 (1993): 471–82.

Snell, John E., Richard J. Rosenwald, and Ames Robey. "The Wifebeater's Wife." *Archives of General Psychiatry* 11, no. 2 (1964): 107–12.

Spitzberg, Brian H., and William R. Cupach. "The State of the Art of Stalking: Taking Stock of the Emerging Literature." *Aggression and Violent Behavior* 12 (2007): 64–86.

Stark, Evan. *Coercive Control: The Entrapment of Women in Personal Life.* New York: Oxford University Press, 2007,

Stark, Evan, and Anne Flitcraft. *Women at Risk: Domestic Violence and Women's Health.* Thousand Oaks, Calif.: Sage, 1996.

Steinmetz, Suzanne K. "The Battered Husband Syndrome." *Victimology* 2, no. 3–4 (1977–78): 499–509.

Stets, Jan E. *Domestic Violence and Control.* New York: Springer-Verlag, 1988.

Stets, Jan E, and Murray A, Straus. "Gender Differences in Reporting Marital Violence and Its Medical and Psychological Consequences." In *Physical Violence in American Families,* edited by Straus and Gelles, 151–65.

———. "The Marriage License as a Hitting License: A Comparison of Assaults in

Dating, Cohabiting, and Married Couples." *Journal of Family Violence* 4, no. 2 (1989): 161–80.

Stith, Sandra M., Karen H. Hosen, Kimberly A. Middleton, Amy L Busch, Kirsten Lundeberg, and Russell. P. Carlton. "The Intergenerational Transmission of Spouse Abuse: A Meta-Analysis." *Journal of Marriage and the Family* 62, no. 3 (2000): 64–54.

Strang, Heather, and John Braithwaite, eds. *Restorative Justice and Family Violence*. Cambridge: Cambridge University Press, 2002.

Straus, Murray A. "The Conflict Tactics Scales and Its Critics: An Evaluation and New Data on Validity and Reliability." In *Physical Violence in American Families*, edited by Straus and Gelles, 49–73.

———. "The Controversy over Domestic Violence by Women: A Methodological, Theoretical, and Sociology of Science Analysis." In *Violence in Intimate Relationships*, edited by Ximena B. Arriaga and Stuart Oskamp, 17–44. Thousand Oaks, Calif.: Sage, 1999.

———. "A General Systems Theory Approach to a Theory of Violence between Family Members." *Social Science Information* 12, no. 3 (1973): 105–25.

———. "Injury and Frequency of Assault and the 'Representative Sample Fallacy' in Measuring Wife Beating and Child Abuse." In *Physical Violence in American Families*, edited by Straus and Gelles, 75–91.

———. "Measuring Intrafamily Conflict and Violence: The Conflict Tactics (CT) Scales." *Journal of Marriage & the Family* 41, no. 1 (1979): 75–88.

———. "Measuring Intrafamily Conflict and Violence: The Conflict Tactics (CT) Scales." In *Physical Violence in American Families*, edited by Straus and Gelles, 29–47.

———. "Prevalence of Violence against Dating Partners by Male and Female University Students Worldwide." *Violence Against Women* 10 (2004): 790–811.

Straus, Murray A., and Richard J. Gelles, eds. *Physical Violence in American Families: Risk Factors and Adaptation to Violence in 8,145 Families*. New Brunswick, N.J.: Transaction Press, 1990.

Straus, Murray A., Richard J. Gelles, and Suzanne K. Steinmetz. *Behind Closed Doors: Violence in the American Family*. Garden City, N.Y.: Doubleday, 1980.

Straus, Murray A., Sherry L. Hamby, Sue Boney-McCoy, and David B. Sugarman. "The Revised Conflict Tactics Scales (CTS2): Development and Preliminary Psychometric Data." *Journal of Family Issues* 17, no. 3 (1996): 283–316.

Straus, Murray A., and Stephen Sweet. "Verbal/Symbolic Aggression in Couples: Incidence Rates and Relationship to Personal Characteristics." *Journal of Marriage and the Family* 54, no. 2 (1992): 346–57.

Sugarman, David B., and Susan L. Frankel. "Patriarchal Ideology and Wife-Assault: A Meta Analytic Review." *Journal of Family Violence* 11, no. 1 (1996): 13–40.

Sullivan, Cris M., and Deborah I. Bybee. "Reducing Violence Using Community-Based Advocacy for Women with Abusive Partners." *Journal of Consulting & Clinical Psychology* 67, no. 1 (1999): 43–53.

Sutherland, Cheryl A., Deborah I. Bybee, and Cris M. Sullivan. "Beyond Bruises and Broken Bones: The Joint Effects of Stress and Injuries on Battered Women's Health." *American Journal of Community Psychology* 30, no.5 (2002): 609–36.

Sutherland, Cheryl Ann. "Investigating the Effects of Intimate Partner Violence in Women's Health (Physical Abuse, Suicide Ideation, Depression)." PhD diss., Michigan State University, 1999.

Sutherland, Cheryl, Deborah Bybee, and Cris Sullivan. "The Long-Term Effects of Battering on Women's Health." *Women's Health: Research on Gender, Behavior, and Policy* 4, no. 1 (1998): 41–70.

Swan, Suzanne C., and David L. Snow. "A Typology of Women's Use of Violence in Intimate Relationships." *Violence against Women* 8, no.3 (2002): 286–319.

Testa, Maria, and Kenneth E. Leonard. "The Impact of Marital Aggression on Women's Psychological and Marital Functioning in a Newlywed Sample." *Journal of Family Violence* 16, no. 2 (2001): 115–30

Tjaden, Patricia, and Nancy Thoennes. *Extent, Nature, and Consequences of Intimate Partner Violence: Findings from the National Violence Against Women Survey.* Research report. Washington, D.C.: National Institute of Justice/Centers for Disease Control and Prevention, 1999.

———. "Prevalence and Consequences of Male-to-Female and Female-to-Male Intimate Partner Violence as Measured by the National Violence Against Women Survey." *Violence Against Women* 6, no. 2 (2000): 142–61.

———. *Violence and Threats of Violence against Women and Men in the United States, 1994–1996.* Ann Arbor, Mich.: Inter-university Consortium for Political and Social Research, 1999.

Tolman, Richard M. "The Validation of Psychological Maltreatment of Women Inventory." Paper presented at the 4th *International Family Violence Conference*, Durham, New Hampshire, 1995.

Tolman, Richard M. "The Development of Measure of Psychological Maltreatment of Women by their Male Partners." *Violence and Victims* 4, no.3 (1989): 159–77.

———. "Psychological Abuse of Women." In *Assessment of Family Violence: A Clinical and Legal Sourcebook,* edited by Robert T. Ammerman and Michael Hersen, 291–310. New York: John Wiley, 1992.

Tweed, Roger G., and Donald G. Dutton. "A Comparison of Impulsive and Instrumental Subgroups of Batterers." *Violence & Victims* 13, no. 3 (1998): 217–30.

United States Department of Justice. Bureau of Justice Statistics, *Intimate Partner Violence, 1993–2001.* Washington, D.C., 2003.

United States Federal Bureau of Investigation. "Crime in the United States 2005." *Uniform Crime Reports.* Washington, D.C., 2006.

ver Steegh, Nancy. "Differentiating Types of Domestic Violence: Implications for Child Custody." *Louisiana Law Review* 65, no. 4 (2005): 1379–431.

Walker, Lenore E. *The Battered Woman.* New York: Harper & Row, 1979.

———. *The Battered Woman Syndrome.* New York: Springer, 1984.

———. "Legal Self-Defense for Battered Women." In *Battering and Family Therapy: A Feminist Perspective,* edited by Marsali Hansen and Michele Harway, 200–16. Thousand Oaks, Calif.: Sage, 1993.

———. *Terrifying Love: Why Battered Women Kill and How Society Responds.* New York: Harper & Row, 1989.

Yllö, Kersti, and Michele Bograd, eds. *Feminist Perspectives on Wife Abuse.* Newbury Park, Calif.: Sage, 1988.

Index

Page numbers in **bold** refer to figures.

advocacy services. *See* public agencies

agencies. *See* public agencies

alcohol, 65, 75, 80, 130n27

antisocial intimate terrorists ("cobras"), 31–33

Archer, John, 88–90, 116n42, 118–19n17

battered husband syndrome, 17, 22–23. *See also* mutuality; women-as-perpetrators

battered wife syndrome. *See* intimate terrorism

Battered Woman, The (Walker), 48

battered woman legal defense, 11. *See also* criminal justice system

battered women's movement. *See* feminism; shelters for battered women

battered women's services. *See* public agencies; shelters for battered women

batterer programs, 78–81, 135n19

Biderman's Chart of Coercion, 14

brainwashing, 14

Browne, Angela, 55–57

Burke, Jessica, 49

Bybee, Deborah, 40

Campbell, Jacquelyn C., 53–54, 103, 121n32

Canadian Violence Against Women Survey, 93

Chang, Valerie, 41

Chicago Women's Health Risk Study (CWHRS), 100–101

child protective services, 81–82

children: custody threats, 15, 54, 88–89; economic dependency and, 38–39, 107; family court and child protective services, 81–82, 126n97; injuries to pregnant women, 40; as risk marker for violence, 36–37, 64–65; violence directed toward, 8, 26, 81–82, 84, 95–96

class. *See* economic status as risk marker

Clements, Kahni, 135n19

cluster analysis, 90–91, 99

coercive control: acts of violence and, 2–3, 9–10, 14, 46–47; as basis for typology of domestic violence, 2–3, 14, 46–47, 117n46, 120n23, 129–30n14; as "liberty crime," 46–47; marriage and, 34–35, 63; measurement of, 16–17, 87–91, 115n39; motive in, 13, 113n10; nonviolent control tactics, 26–29; overview, 13–17, 47; Power and Control Wheel, **7**, 7–8; sexual control, 96; sustained "ownership" as goal of, 6, 13; "violent coercive control" term, 126n97; web of abuse, 9. *See also* economic abuse; intimidation; stalking; surveillance

Coercive Control Scale, 115n39

cohabiting couples, 34–35, 63. *See also* intimate relationships

Cohan, Catherine L., 127n11

common couple violence, 115n36. *See also* situational couple violence

communication skills, 66–67, 80, 82

Conflict Tactics Scales, 98, 108, 112–13n9, 114–15n34

Controlling Behaviors Scale, 88–89
coordinated community response, 83,
133n7
criminal justice system: alternative sentencing, 77; arrest and prosecution
policies, 76–77, 133–34n10; battered
woman defense, 11; gender disparities
in, 55; marital rights and, 34–35;
Protection from Abuse orders, 19–21,
20–22, 73, 76; restorative justice
compared with, 77–78; sampling
data from, 20–21, **20–22**, 25; "self-
defense" concept in, 51–52, 127n14;
situational couple violence and, 19;
typology of domestic violence and,
75–77, 134n12. *See also* Protection
from Abuse orders
cycle of violence, 49

Davies, Lyon, 133–34n10
dependent intimate terrorists ("pit
bulls"), 31–33
depression, 42
destruction of property, 15
Dobash, Rebecca and Russell, 14,
26–27, 41
domestic violence, 6, 79–80, 111n2. *See
also* intimate terrorism; typology of
domestic violence
drugs, 65, 75
Duluth Domestic Abuse Intervention
Project, 7–8. *See also* Power and
Control Wheel
Dutton, Mary Ann, 14–15, 87–88,
117–18n4
dysphoric/borderline batterer, 31–33

Eckhardt, Christopher I., 134–35n18
economic abuse: coercive control and,
88–90; overview, 16, 38–39; financial
independence intervention strategies,
75; gender disparities in resources,
55; measurement of, 95; Pittsburgh

data on, 28; as Power and Control
Wheel element, **7**, 8
economic status as risk marker, 63, 68,
75, 130n16. *See also* economic abuse
education as risk marker, 35–36, 68
Effects of Violence on Work and Family
Study, 39, 51, 97–99
emotional abuse, 9, 96. *See also*
psychological health
emotional dependency, 32, 79
equifinality, 113n10
ethnicity as risk marker, 36. *See also* race
as risk marker

family court, 81–82, 126n97
family history as risk marker, 34, 68,
121–22n35, 131n34
fear and anxiety, 41–42, 43,
124nn73–74. *See also* intimidation
feminism: attention to coercive control
in, 2–3, 14; batterer programs and,
79–80; criminal justice system and,
55, 128n26, 133–34n10; family violence scholarship and, 18–19, 114n28;
feminist research on resistance,
117n1; gender theory and, 54–55, 105;
male attitudes toward women as violence factor, 31–32, 106; prevention
initiatives and, 84; second wave feminist research, 25; shelters for battered
women and, 73, 132n3; woman-
defined advocacy, 133–34n10. *See also*
gender
Ferraro, Kathleen, 34, 49–50
Fisher, Ellen R., 49
Frankel, Susan L., 32, 106, 120nn26–27
Frieze, Irene, 19

Gartner, Rosemary, 35, 122n40,
129–30n14
Gelles, Richard, 61
gender: gendered division of labor, 65,
130n23; gender symmetry in violence,

3, 22–23, 108–9, 111n9, 116n42; as institution, 54–55, 105; intimate terrorism and, 105–9. *See also* feminism; male privilege; same-sex relationships

generally violent/antisocial batterer, 31–33

Golding, Jacqueline, 42

Gondolf, Edward W., 49

Goodman, Lisa, 14–15, 87–88, 117–18n4

Gottman, John, 32–33, 121n29

Graham-Kevan, Nicola, 88–90, 116n42, 118–19n17

help-seeking, 42, 51, 127n11

Holtzworth-Munroe, Amy, 31–33, 67, 106, 120nn23–24

homicidal resistance, 55–59, **58**

incipient intimate terrorism, 46–47, 103, 126n97

injuries. *See* physical health

intergenerational transmission, 34, 68, 121–22n35, 131n34

intervention strategies: batterer programs, 78–81, 135n19; coordinated community response, 83, 133n7; couples counseling, 75; family court and child protective services, 81–82, 126n97; overview, 72–86; prevention initiatives, 83–84; restorative justice, 77–78. *See also* criminal justice system; public agencies; shelters for battered women

intimate homicide, 57–59, **58**, 121n32

intimate partner violence, 111n2

intimate relationships: communication skills in, 66–67, 80, 82; conflict in, 62–67; couples counseling, 75; effects of abuse on, 43–45; marriage as violence marker, 34–35, 63, 122n40; parenting issues in, 81–82; separa-

tion-precipitated violence, 46, 64, 102–4. *See also* cohabiting couples; marriage; same-sex relationships

intimate terrorism: defined, 2–3, 111n2, 117–18n4, 117n2, 126n97; effects of, 37–45; gender and, 105–7; incipient intimate terrorism, 46–47, 103, 126n97; injuries reported from, 39–41, 118–19n17; intervention strategies for, 73–75, 78–81; mutual violence in, 30; overview, 5–10, **6**; "patriarchal terrorism" term for, 115n36; psychological health and, 41–43; risk markers for, 33–37; sampling data on, **20–22**, 20–23, 90–91, 115–16nn39–41, 116–17n45, 129n9; types of intimate terrorists, 31–33, 67, 120n23, 121n29, 131n35, 134–35n18; "violent coercive control" term for, 126n97

intimidation: coercive control and, 15; fear and anxiety, 41–42, 43, 124nn73–74; female vs. male physical size differential and, 106–8; measurement of, 87–90, 94–95; nonviolent tactics of, 26–27; as Power and Control Wheel element, **7**, 9; threats of violence, 53–54

isolation, 8–9, 50–51, 96

Jacobson, Neil, 32–33, 121n29

jealousy, 32

Johnston, Janet R., 103

Kantor, Glenda Kaufman, 130n27

Kirkwood, Catherine: on coercive control tactics, 26; on fear as motivation for self-reliance, 42; on self-esteem, 41; on strategies for escaping abuse, 45, 54; on the "web of abuse," 9

Laroche, Denis, 116n42, 118–19n17, 119n20

law enforcement. *See* criminal justice system

learned helplessness theory, 133–34n10

leaving violent relationships: decline in violent resistance and, 59, 128n26, 128n31; financial independence and, 75; overview, 53–55; separation-precipitated violence and, 46, 64, 102–4; strategies for escaping abuse, 45, 48, 54. *See also* resistance

legitimation, 15–16, 88–89

Leonard, Kenneth E., 43–44

Leone, Janel M., 39–40, 51, 127n11

Macmillan, Ross, 35, 122n40, 129–30n14

male privilege: alcohol and, 130n27; economic abuse and, 8; legitimation and, 88–89; marriage as basis for, 14, 107; measurement of, 95; men's attitudes as risk factor, 31–32, 120nn26–27; "patriarchal terrorism" term, 115n36. *See also* gender

marital rape, 14

marriage, 34–35, 63, 122n40. *See also* intimate relationships

mental health. *See* depression; psychological health; self-esteem

methodology: bias in sampling data, 18–19, **20–22**, 51, 115–16nn39–40; cluster analysis, 90–91, 99, 116n41; coercive control score, 16–17, 115n39; cross-sectional vs. longitudinal approaches, 37; differential effects studies, 94–100; interpretation of biased data, 12–13, 23–24, 85, 91–92; survey question practices, 13, 112–13n9, 133n8; terminology, 111n2, 112n2, 112n4, 115n36, 120n23, 126n97

Miller, Susan, 52, 127n14

Mills, Linda, 78, 133–34n10

minimizing, denying, and blaming, 9

money (in intimate relationships). *See* economic abuse; economic status as risk marker

monitoring of partner's behavior, 15, 27–29, 102–4

mutuality, 29–30, 76–77. *See also* battered husband syndrome; symmetry; women-as-perpetrators

mutual violent control, 5, **6**, 11–12, 20–22, **20–22**, 117n2

National Family Violence Survey: on alcohol correlation with violence, 65; Battered Husband Syndrome data from, 17–18; on conflict correlation with violence, 66; on family income correlation with violence, 64; family violence approach and, 18–19, 63, 84, 114n28; on fear and anxiety, 42; on gender symmetry, 108; on situational couple violence, 61–63, 69–70; violent acts described in, 130n17

NVAW Survey (National Violence Against Women Survey): injuries reported in, 39; overview, 93–94; on psychological health, 42, 69–70; on risk markers, 35–36, 68, 122–23nn47–49

Olson, Lenore, 67, 131n34

Pagelow, Mildred D., 51, 53

passivity, 48–49

patriarchal terrorism, 115n36. *See also* intimate terrorism

patriarchal tradition. *See* male privilege

Paymar, Michael, 14, 88–89, 94

Pence, Ellen, 14, 88–89, 94

personality characteristics of violent men, 67, 79

physical health: comparison of injuries from the types of domestic violence, 40; injuries from intimate terrorism,

39–41, 118–19nn17–19; injuries from sexual abuse, 40; injuries from situational couple violence, 39, 62, 69, 70–71, 118–19nn17–19; injuries to pregnant women, 40; intimate homicide, 57–59, **58**; overview, 39–41

Physical Violence Scale, 99

Pittsburgh data: on chronic intimate terrorism, 129n9; cluster analysis of, 90–91; on effects of violence on relationships, 44–45; on fear and anxiety, 41; in-depth results from, 37; injuries reported in, 39, 69; methodology of, 19–21; mutual violent control reported in, 117n2; nonviolent control tactics reported in, 27; overview, 92–93; risk marker data from, 34–36, 122n42; on situational couple violence, 61–62, 69; women-as-perpetrator data from, 29–30

post-traumatic stress syndrome, 42, 91

Power and Control Scale, 101

Power and Control Wheel: batterer programs and, 79–80; development of, 14; measurement of coercive control and, 88–89; overview, **7**, 7–8; relation to controlling violence, 16; typology of domestic violence and, 73–74

prevention initiatives, 83–84

Protection from Abuse orders, 19–21, **20–22**, 73, 76, 133n7. See also criminal justice system

psychological health: emotional abuse, 9, 96; intimate terrorism and, 41–43; restorative justice and, 77–78; satisfaction from intimate relationships, 44–45; self-esteem, 27–28, 41, 48–49, 88–90; situational couple violence and, 69–71

Psychological Maltreatment of Women Inventory (PMWI), 89, 120n23

public agencies: breadth of social service network, 43; children and,

81–82; sampling data from, 19–21, **20–22**, 25; typology of domestic violence implications for, 73–75; women's help-seeking practices, 51, 127n11

race as risk marker, 36, 68, 122–23nn47–49. See also ethnicity as risk marker

rape, 14

relationships. See intimate relationships; same-sex relationships

resistance: feminist research on, 117n1; overview, 49–51; sampling data on, 51; survivor theory, 49, 133–34n10; undermining resistance, 15–16, 27–29, 53, 88–89. See also leaving violent relationships; public agencies; shelters for battered women; violent resistance

restorative justice, 77–78

Riger, Stephanie, 39

risk markers, 33–37, 63, 67–68, 120nn26–27, 121n32. See also particular risk markers

Russell, Diana, 14

safety plans, 73–74

same-sex relationships, 25, 85, 109, 112n4, 113n13, 115n36. See also gender; intimate relationships

Saunders, Daniel, 42, 79

self-defense, 51–52, 127n14

self-esteem, 27–28, 41, 48–49, 88–90

separation-precipitated violence, 46, 64, 102–4

sexual abuse, 40

sexual control, 96

sexuality, 44, 63

sexually transmitted disease, 40

shelters for battered women: breadth of network of, 43; sampling data from, 19–21, **20–22**, 133n8; typology of

shelters for battered women (*continued*)
domestic violence implications for,
73–75; woman-defined advocacy and,
133–34n10; women's help-seeking
practices, 42, 51, 127n11

situational couple violence: actors in situational couple violence, 31; chronic
situational couple violence, 62–68,
129n11; "common couple violence"
term and, 115n36; custody of children
and, 81–82; defined, 5; economic
abuse and, 28; family income correlation with, 64; gender and, 107–9;
homicide in, 121n32; injuries reported from, 39, 62, 69, 70–71,
118–19n17; intervention strategies
for, 74–75, 78–80; intimate terrorism
compared with, 19–20; mutual
violence in, 30; overview, **6**, 11–12,
60–62; psychological health and,
69–71; sampling data on, **20–22**,
20–23, 90–91, 115–16nn39–41,
116–17n45; typological approach and,
2–3; variability of, 70–71; violent acts
and, 29; violent resistance distinguished from, 53, 127n14, 127n18

social class. *See* economic status as risk
marker

social service agencies. *See* public
agencies

stalking, 45, 54, 102–4. *See also*
surveillance

Stark, Evan, 14, 46–47, 91, 126n97

Steinmetz, Suzanne, 17

Stets, Jan E., 69–70

Stith, Sandra M., 34

Straus, Murray A., 61–62, 69–70,
130n27

Sugarman, David B., 32, 106,
120nn26–27

suicide, 57

Sullivan, Cris, 40, 43

surveillance, 15, 27–29, 102–4. *See also*
stalking

survivor theory, 49, 133–34n10

Sutherland, Cheryl, 40, 43

symmetry (gender symmetry in domestic violence), 3, 22–23, 108–9, 111n9,
116n42. *See also* mutuality; women-as-
perpetrators

Testa, Maria, 43–44

Thoennes, Nancy, 122n47

threats. *See* intimidation

Tjaden, Patricia, 122n47

Tolman, Richard M., 89, 120n23

typology of domestic violence: battered
husband syndrome and, 18; comparison of effects on relationships, 44;
comparison of victims' injuries, 40;
control context as basis for, 2–3, 14,
46–47, 117n46, 120n23, 129–30n14;
feminist approaches and, 73; impli-
cation for intervention, 72–86; interpretation of biased data and, 12–13,
23–24, 85, 91–92; overview, 3–4;
personality characteristics of violent
men and, 67, 79; role of physical
violence in, 91. *See also particular types
of domestic violence*

verbal aggression, 66

Violence Screening Tool, 100–101

violent acts: as basis for typology of
domestic violence, 14, 122n40,
129–30n14; coercive control and,
2–3, 9–10, 14; correlation with homicidal resistance, 55–56; female vs.
male physical size differential and,
106–8; intimate homicide, **58;** marriage and, 34–35, 63; measurement
of, 98, 100–101, 114–15n34, 118–
19nn17–19, 130n17; nature and pattern of, 29–30. *See also* physical health

violent coercive control, 126n97

violent resistance: custody of children and, 81–82; decline in incidence of, 59, 128n26, 128n31; defined, 5, **6;** homicidal resistance, 55–59, **58;** mandated-arrest policies and, 76; mutual violent control distinguished from, 12; overview, 10–11, 51–53; "perpetrator" term and, 112n2; sampling data on, **20–22,** 20–22, 30; as "self-defense," 51–52, 127n14; situational couple violence distinguished from, 53, 127n14, 127n18; suicide, 57

Walker, Lenore, 48–49, 133–34n10

web of abuse, 9

wife beating, 121–22n35

woman-defined advocacy, 133–34n10

women-as-perpetrators: battered husband syndrome debate, 17–23; gender symmetry debate and, 3, 22–23, 108–9, 111n9, 116n42; law enforcement treatment of, 76–77; "perpetrator" vs. "resistor" terms, 112n2; statistical data on, 1–2, **21,** 29–30; women as intimate terrorists, 112n4, 115n36, 119n20. *See also* mutuality; symmetry